INDIAN TERRITORY

INDIAN TERRITORY

A Frontier Photographic Record by W. S. Prettyman

Selected and edited by Robert E. Cunningham

NORMAN

UNIVERSITY OF OKLAHOMA PRESS

► FRONTISPIECE: *Washunga of the Kaws*

Library of Congress Catalog Card Number: 57–11192
Copyright 1957 by the University of Oklahoma Press
Publishing Division of the University
Composed and printed at Norman, Oklahoma, U.S.A.
By the University of Oklahoma Press
First edition, October, 1957
Second printing, September, 1958

To Jeanie, my wife
whose patience and help
are essential in all things

FOREWORD

IT SEEMED an innocent enough hobby to collect early photographs of Oklahoma, particularly when one small drawer could hold the lot. The first of these pictures went into the drawer, when, as a newspaper reporter, I undertook to interview as many pioneer settlers of Oklahoma as possible and write about their experiences. That was in the early 1930's when there were quite a few left of those who had made the original "run" into Oklahoma Territory in 1889. They were still young enough to have good memories and old enough to enjoy sharing them. Each seemed to have one or more treasured pictures, some with the sepia coloring faded and the cardboard corners roughed by wear. The younger members of the pioneer families seemed to have little interest in these old pictures, and the owners were willing to part with them to have them saved.

Over the years the need for more space became apparent. My photographic background suggested also the collection of original plates, made by pioneer photographers, from which better prints for reproduction could be obtained. This was a more difficult undertaking, but systematic search in logical places uncovered more than ten thousand fragile glass negatives that had survived fires, storms, and periodic house cleanings. Some tragic accounts could be related of the valuable collections missed by only a few weeks or a few months.

The unending task of identification and cataloging was helped little by the photographers. A few had scratched identification in the emulsion of their plates. All the books, pamphlets, newspapers, and other materials published during or about the period photographed had to be studied, but gradually a measure of order began to appear.

More than fifty photographers were identified as participants in this collection. They were men of varying capabilities. Some captured only an incident, some an event, some a larger slice of history.

Yet all were significant, for here was the crisp truth of the past, unchangeable by time or the retelling from faulty memory. Here were no artists' conceptions sketched after the event or shaped for composition; here no individual impressions but actual pictures of the people and places exactly as the photographers found them. The West is older than the photographer, but this phase of the West was born as the camera watched.

The age of pictorial journalism was in the future when most of these photographs were made. The halftone screen and relief etching of photographs did not come into general use until the last decade of the nineteenth century. Prints made by the most careful craftsmen survived the waiting period, but even the fading of an old print presents no problem when the original plate is available.

Years of association with such a varied collection makes each plate a close friend, and sorting them makes each photographer more than a casual acquaintance. It was little short of startling to watch the work of one man emerge from the assortment and entitle him to extra consideration. His astounding contribution could not be just a part of a picture story, although it fitted neatly into the sequence. His plates could speak alone and tell a story with great eloquence. This man had photographed an epoch. He was William S. Prettyman.

His kind of story was hardly new to history, although it had perhaps not been told this way. It was an account of a primitive people, living in a manner and with traditions little changed by the centuries, invaded by a more advanced and better armed civilization that forced its will on this lesser society and accelerated its progress beyond its capacity to adjust. Plutarch tells this kind of story many times, as do Herodotus and the Latin and medieval historians who relate the invasion of the present British Isles by the Romans, Saxons, and Scandinavians.

Prettyman saw "squaw patches"—little plots of corn or squashes —he could leap over expand to fields he could not see across. He watched tipis give way to stone buildings, while his bewildered Indian friends tried to understand. Enough of his carefully made photographic record remains to describe this epoch, almost without words.

Like a Persian weaver, he worked from the reverse side of his rug and was not permitted to see the pattern he created. But he chose his colors in a careful sequence, providing a design that slights no detail. He seemed to arrive just in time to picture each portion of the pageant of civilization as it took place. The Indians were soon to abandon their primitive state. Shortly after Prettyman pictured the bark lodges of the Sacs and the Kaws, they disappeared, to be seen no more. The sacred dances of the Poncas were abandoned on government order.

Cowboy camps and vast ranges, the second phase of changing civilization, were gone almost as soon as they were photographed. The Boomers, who formed the advance guard of the coming white settlers, were fleeting actors on this great stage, and finally the homesteader arrived with his pathetic assortment of implements to conquer the prairie.

The era of settlement was even more unstable than those that preceded it. Every day brought more change, as progress forced outmoded ways to disappear. A photographer had to work fast, and be in many places, to tell this story. Prettyman ended his task only when the new land was taking the pattern of the rest of the nation. Everywhere else in the world the story of civilization had taken centuries to unfold. Here, on the Oklahoma prairies, it happened in one lifetime, and one man recorded most of it in photographs.

Prettyman's work has not been overlooked entirely, although there are photographs in this book which will not have been seen before by present-day readers—pictures so old they are new. The book on Oklahoma that does not contain some of his pictures is rare, and there are living pioneers who remember him. In 1933 George Rainey published a privately printed book, *The Cherokee Strip,* which contained this paragraph:

> "Before the opening of Oklahoma to white settlement, one W. S. Prettyman, photographer, installed a photographing outfit in a covered wagon to which he hitched two yoke of oxen, and with this toured much of the then wild and virgin country. This man made photographs of many objects of historical value and interest."

Two old friends who have been helpful in many ways in supplying background information for my collection knew Prettyman. One was the son of the government blacksmith at the Sac and Fox agency, who remembered a pleasant boyhood at that place. Years ago he urged me to make a special effort to find pictures "made by a man named Prettyman," a favorite among the Indians. The other was the son of a licensed trader with the Osages, who stated that Prettyman pictures were needed in any collection on early-day Oklahoma.

Mr. Ray T. Prettyman, one of the photographer's three sons, who lived in retirement in Pasadena, California, made a special trip to Oklahoma recently to assist in every way possible in the preparation of this book. He brought along his father's scrap book, his favorite album with careful identification, and a supply of memories filled with anecdotes and accounts of the experiences of his father. He also had a family genealogical chart that dates back to the sixteenth century. His help was invaluable.

There were others, many of them, who supplied needed information, one of whom I will mention by name. She is Mrs. Alpha Skirving, a resident of Blackwell, Oklahoma, the daughter of a prominent pioneer, herself a school teacher and a patient collector of Prettyman material. She has spent years gathering everything obtainable on this illustrious former resident. Her plan is to establish a Prettyman museum in Blackwell where the photographer may be re-discovered by new generations. She has made available all her material and has assisted greatly in furthering this work.

One of the pleasantest experiences in my research was the showing of many of these pictures to Indians. Eyes dimmed by age brightened when they saw the likenesses of friends and relatives long gone. Only the very old remembered these faces. Not one living Indian is pictured in this book, and without the help of these elderly people more would have to remain unknown forever. Prettyman was not one to preserve careful identification of all his pictures. He was a photographer by design, and a historian only by chance.

Robert E. Cunningham

Stillwater, Oklahoma

June 1, 1957

CONTENTS

INDIAN TERRITORY

1. William S. Prettyman, Photographer

When he joined the western migration in 1879, William S. Prettyman was too filled with the thought of adventure to be concerned about his meagre purse. Besides, he was only 21 years old and felt able to cope with any problem. Thousands of others were making the same journey, some burdened with years and large families.

His English ancestors had come to America in 1638, to be among the earliest pioneers. Primitive ways and life with the stone age people who then populated the slopes and valleys of Delaware were a part of their existence. Two centuries later, Prettyman's parents lived in Princess Anne county, Maryland, where, on November 12, 1858, William was born.

By the time the Civil War had ended and young William was old enough to enjoy the stories of Indians and pioneers, Maryland had changed. Early primitive life was beyond the memory of the oldest residents, but there still was a mysterious frontier beyond the great river which men of Maryland visited and from which they brought back glowing accounts of adventure. As he grew to manhood, William Prettyman felt the common urge of young men to go west, and shortly after his twenty-first birthday he stepped off the train at Emporia, Kansas, with five cents in his pocket. He used this money to buy a post card and stamp to announce his safe arrival to relatives back home.

He tried a number of odd jobs to earn food and lodging before he found a profession completely strange but extremely fascinating. He became an apprentice to a Civil War photographer, I. H. Bonsall, who operated a gallery in Arkansas City, Kansas. This was to become his life's work, and it was to be his privilege to add dignity to this relatively new profession, as well as to make a monumental contribution to history.

3

When Bonsall came to Kansas after the Civil War, photography was new in the West. For nearly half a century the great open spaces, the colorful inhabitants of the region, and the adventure there, had belonged to artists. George Catlin, Alfred Jacob Miller, Seth Eastman, Carl Bodmer, Charles Deas, and others had brought the living West to the world, but with the misty element of imagination and individual impression. Then such men as William H. Jackson, L. A. Huffman, D. F. Barry, and others began to picture the disappearing West with the awkward photographic equipment that was the best of the time. They captured realism that time and faulty memories could not distort. This was a dedicated profession, but Bonsall was too old to join their ranks. He kept busy picturing the town and area where he settled, but in Prettyman he produced a man of the stature of Jackson and Huffman with the youth and vision to make certain that this part of the equally exciting West was not overlooked.

Prettyman did not begin where the others stopped, for he did his best work during the same years his famous contemporaries were most active. He did pick up the thread of the Indian story from them, but at the point where the hostile Indians moved out of their wildest state, and off the dripping collodian plates of Barry and Huffman, into an entirely new atmosphere, with a new attitude born of necessity.

Prettyman was not long in mastering the rudiments of portrait photography, and in a short time opened his own gallery. It was a success from the start. Over the years he photographed almost every important person in the Middle West. He delighted in making pictures of war veterans, some still wearing remnants of their blue and grey uniforms. He pictured the pioneer women in their sunbonnets, at their spinning wheels, and ladies obviously conscious of their top-heavy Fifth Avenue hats. He photographed outlaws, sometimes without being aware of their profession. Bob Dalton, who died in a gun battle with the citizens of Coffeyville, Kansas, was one of his subjects.

"When he came into the gallery he had on his revolver and belt," Prettyman recalled. "He pulled out his six-shooter and laid it on the wash stand in the dressing room. In combing his hair he used so much water that it prevented his hair from photographing well. I objected with very strong language. He appeared so nervous that he had to have a head rest to remain steady during the exposure."

The photograph made was that of a smooth-faced young man of nineteen or twenty. At the time he was a deputy United States marshal in the Osage Nation. He ordered a dozen cabinet-sized, three-quarter length pictures, to be sent to the Osage Agency. When Dalton became an outlaw the picture became a collector's item. A collector of outlaw material obtained one of these prints and brought it to Prettyman to be copied, claiming that it was the only one in existence and an extremely valuable property. Prettyman went to his files and produced the original glass plate from which the print was made. Later Prettyman was to make another photograph of Dalton, this time lying dead with three others of his wild bunch on a hayrack in Coffeyville.

After he had opened his gallery in Arkansas City, a group of Osage Indians came to him for a picture. These tall, big-framed Indians with roached hairdress had come from below the Flint Hills Escarpment that spilled over into northeastern Indian Territory from Kansas. In early historic times they had occupied land in Kansas, on the Neosho, and still earlier they had ranged, as one of the great divisions of the Siouan group, as far north and east as St. Louis, and had been able to dominate a vast territory from the Mississippi to the Great Plains.

This was the first of several pictures of the Osages and the beginning of a new interest for Prettyman. To photograph an Indian in a studio was like picturing an eagle in a cage, and he, like all others who knew the red man in his proper element, envisioned a better treatment for such subjects. He had seen Indians in their wild state when he served for a brief period as a photographer in a military campaign against the Apaches. On this expedition he examined the body of a close friend who had been captured and mutilated by these Indians. Only by a miracle and a fast horse was Prettyman himself able to escape a like fate.

He came away from this experience with his scalp, but without any enduring hatred for the red race. In fact, he was quite willing to take a chance with the Indians who occupied the Indian Territory to the south, in order to make a final record before the pending fusion of the races left the old ways buried in history. He could go in any direction and find interesting subjects, for almost one-third of all the Indians on the North American continent lived in what is now Oklahoma.

Many changes had taken place in the Indian Territory during Prettyman's lifetime. In the year of his birth, 1858, it belonged primarily to the Five Civilized Tribes, the Cherokees, Chickasaws, Choctaws, Seminoles, and Creeks, who had come from Georgia, Florida, Alabama, Mississippi, and the Carolinas, much against their will, to this little known land, believed in 1830 to be too far west ever to be wanted by white settlers. In the latter year the Indian Removal Act was passed, forcing these advanced tribesmen to remove to this area west of the Mississippi. Three decades later, they had become adjusted and reasonably happy in their new environment, only to suffer the disruptions of the American Civil War. One of the dramatic aftermaths of the war was the movement of thousands of whites westward into the Trans-Mississippi region, of which the Indian Territory was a part.

The Indians there were not to escape the consequences of the war or the migration that followed it. Since many members of the Five Civilized Tribes had served in the Confederate Army, they were classed by the federal government as enemies. Their Confederate allegiance cancelled, in fact, existing treaties. New agreements were forced upon them which took away more than one-half of their original holdings. The land thus gained by the government was to be used to relocate minor tribes from other areas now standing in the way of a westward migration that promised to occupy every useful acre on the continent.

The Five Civilized Tribes pulled back, to confine life and activities to the rugged eastern half of the Indian Territory. Only the Cherokees, who occupied the northeastern corner of the Territory, kept land that penetrated the western domain. It was an area fifty-eight miles wide that extended westward below the Kansas line to the buffalo prairies east of the Rocky Mountains, and was known as the Cherokee Outlet.

South of the Cherokee Nation were the Creeks and Seminoles, and still farther south were the great domains of the Choctaws and Chickasaws which extended to the brown waters of the Red River. All this was good Indian country, coursed by clear, quick streams, and dotted with broad, fertile valleys. The rugged Kiamichis, Winding Stair and Sans Bois mountains, and the Ozark foothills filled the historic mission of discouraging plundering enemy hordes as well as to slow the penetration of alien cultures. Older Indians of these tribes who could remember the homeland of their ancestors east of the Great River could find similarities and draw favorable comparisons between this new land and the areas they had left.

The movement of nomadic tribes into the millions of acres on the western plains vacated by federal action against the Five Tribes began almost immediately. The once great tribes of the Sac and Fox Indians were among the first to move. They had occupied fertile land in Kansas, and were quick to feel the pressure of the immigration tide. In 1869 a commission was sent from Washington to find suitable land for these people in the Indian Territory. A report of the commission included these words:

> "The Sac and Fox tribes desire to remove to their new home early this coming fall, so soon as their crops can be gathered. Already the settlers are crowding upon this diminished reserve in Kansas, although by treaty they are to remain in undisturbed possession until they are removed to their new homes. In many instances the settlers have moved into the Indian houses, driving the occupants from them."

The Pawnees came willingly. Although their roots were deep in the fertile soil along the Loup Fork of the Platte, they were at constant war with their Sioux neighbors to the northwest. Only the Pawnees had the numerical and moral strength to oppose these lords of the plains, but in 1874 a band on a buffalo hunt was overwhelmed by a Sioux war party, and more than one thousand Pawnees died, most of them women and children. That year the Pawnees began their southward movement, taking with them an array of Sioux scalps, a number of captives, and an enduring hatred for that tribe.

They settled in a rugged area south of the Osages, the Arkansas

River forming the boundary between them, and the Cimarron River was the south line. New diet, water, and climate took a heavy toll during the first years the Pawnees lived in the Territory, but their hatred for the Sioux survived.

In 1876, General Philip Henry Sheridan instructed Major Frank North to recruit a Pawnee battalion of scouts for service against the Sioux during the outbreak which ended with the Battle of Little Bighorn. Only one hundred men could be taken, although every Pawnee warrior wanted to enlist. After the selected few left by wagon from the agency for the railroad station at Coffeyville, Kansas, to entrain for the battle zone, many of those left behind walked all the way to Coffeyville, urged on by the hope that some of those selected might be unable to make the trip. The scouts returned in 1877 after performing spectacular service. One youthful warrior, Rush Roberts, outlived every other participant in the Sioux wars.

Located in the Cherokee Outlet, along with the Pawnees and Osages, and west of them, were the Ponca, Otoe, and Missouri tribes, and the decimated Tonkawas, west of the Poncas. The Kansa, or Kaw Indians, were a few miles northwest of these tribes, their small reservation touching the Kansas border. Here began the plateau, or plains country that extended westward to the foothills of the Rockies. These treeless miles stretched endlessly to the north, south and west, broken only by temperamental streams that flooded and fallowed with the seasons. A rank growth of tall grass marked this land for buffalo and, later, for enormous herds of cattle.

These lesser tribes had come, like the Pawnees, from the north, with the single exception of the Tonkawas, who had ventured up from the south, and had been almost annihilated en route by the Southern Plains Indians. They appealed to the military for help, and the remnants found a home at last.

Far to the west in the Indian Territory were the Southern Cheyennes and Arapahoes, who had come down from Kansas and Nebraska to live on the flat plains, in the pathway of migrant buffalo. Near by were the Wichitas and Caddos. In the land to the south, extending to the Red River, were the Comanches, Kiowas, and Apaches, who had come in reluctantly from the salt plains of Texas and the

8

staked plains farther to the west. This rugged land in Oklahoma, part of their historic range, provided the ideal base of operations for these marauders in their depredations against the Texans.

Crowded into the central portion of the Territory were several tribes, the Iowas, Sacs and Foxes, Kickapoos, Potawatomis, and Shawnees. This area was a mixture of woodland and fertile valleys, habitat of wild game and offering excellent opportunities for agriculture.

In the extreme northeast, inside the old borders of the Cherokee Nation, were the Quapaws, Peorias, Ottawas, Shawnees, Modocs, Wyandottes, and Senecas, small tribes gathered here and there, some from the East, often from the far West.

As is the case with all patchwork construction, some material was unused when the final relocation was completed. This time the residue was approximately two million acres of good land in almost the exact center of the Territory. It was called at first "The Unassigned Lands," since it was assigned to no tribes when it seemed as though the shuffling process had at last reached an end. Here was the Achilles' heel in the Indian fortress that eventually opened the way to white settlement in this by-passed land, the destruction of tribal government, and the obliteration of Indian culture.

Around the Indian Territory were areas where white settlers could come and go at will. In Kansas, to the north, Arkansas to the east, Texas to the south, and Colorado to the northwest, white men could build homes and cities, till the soil, buy and sell their holdings. Even in New Mexico Territory, to the west, restrictions against white settlement were no barrier. While these surrounding states and one territory were not fully occupied, the barrier of Indian borders made the grass greener inside the forbidden area. While Kansas and Missouri pleaded for more settlers, and offered opportunities superior in many ways to those inside the Indian Territory, whites clamored for admission to this last restricted land.

The propaganda that precedes every assault was colored with the virtues and possibilities of this great Territory. Glowing accounts made no mention of hardship, and it is no wonder that strong men who knew about chinch bugs in Kansas, or mosquitoes in Missouri and Arkansas, would have their heads turned by glowing accounts that glossed over the adversity that dulls the ardor of every frontier settlement.

Lexicographers already had admitted a new word to the dictionaries, "Boomers." These were the prophets of plenty who had been the vanguard of the advancing frontier. They led men across the Rocky Mountains in 1849 to Sutter's Mill, into the Black Hills in 1875, both times for gold. They "boomed" and boosted new settlements and new opportunities across the nation, all too often for their own financial gain.

In the Middle West in the 1880's the term was remembered, but more generally applied. Anyone who advocated the opening of the Indian Territory to white settlement, and eventually almost anyone who traveled in a covered wagon, was referred to as a Boomer, particularly if he had designs on a quarter-section of land in the Indian Territory.

The most militant of the Boomer leaders appeared frequently before Prettyman's camera. He was David L. Payne, a Civil War veteran, soldier in the Indian campaigns, frontier scout, Kansas lawmaker, and finally a doorkeeper in the House of Representatives in Washington. Prettyman watched with detached interest as Payne fired his followers with a desire to invade the Indian stronghold, and turn the fertile acres to better account. On the shaded banks of the river south of Arkansas City a Boomer audience could be found almost anytime, and Payne was both a willing and able speaker. A particularly remembered phrase, which Prettyman thought enough of to record, was this Biblical quotation used frequently by Payne: "The Lord commandeth unto Moses: Go forth and possess the Promised Land."

The cattlemen who grazed their herds on Indian land under government sanction were Payne's chief target. He contended homesteaders should have equal rights. Ranchers entered the Territory "through the back door," at a time when their product was needed in the meat-hungry East. The Civil War had closed the normal channels of trade between North and South, and after Appomattox there was a scarcity of meat in the East when there was a surplus of fat steers in Texas. The Indian Territory blocked the way to market, but not for long. Opportunity for profit caused ranchers to dare the hostility of the Indians and wrath of the government to drive their cattle to the railheads in Kansas for shipment to eastern markets.

Over the years millions of longhorns walked the western trails, fattening on the lush grass as they crossed the Indian Territory. Indians consented to this temporary use of their land for a small fee, and occasional levies of beeves from passing herds. Permanent leases of Indian land was the next logical step, and great ranches suddenly flourished on the Indian plains.

As early as 1883 Prettyman had heard the ominous rumblings, which also reached legislative halls in Washington, and gave clear warning that white settlers soon would spread over the land of the Indians. On the Kansas border the pending invasion was even more obvious, and Prettyman watched Boomer groups disappear from time to time into the Territory, only to return shortly thereafter under military escort. He had little sympathy for these people, a feeling not shared generally by the Kansas merchants. The latter wished to see their trade territory extended to the south, a prospect which could only be realized if this vast land was broken into family-sized holdings.

Sensing that there was little time left for him to picture Indians in their natural setting, Prettyman decided upon a one-man invasion of the Territory. He planned cautiously at first, calling his trip a vacation and hunting expedition, but he stowed a camera and a supply of plates in his canvas-covered spring wagon. His associates were to operate his gallery during his absence.

One beautiful September morning in 1883 he trotted his mules down Summit Street and across the long bridge over the Arkansas River. The short stretch of Kansas land in front of him was quickly traversed, and the unknown beckoned. To Prettyman's left, across the river that penetrated deep into the Territory, was the rutted trail known as the Agency Road. Angling off to the southwest was the less traveled Traders' Trail that would take him to the Ponca Agency. He chose neither for this trip.

This was to be an adventure as well as a vacation; an escape from the narrow confines of his darkroom and a chance to cure the sting of acetic acid fumes in his nostrils with clean, pure air. The mules caught the challenge and needed little urging to quit the trail and plow into the tall grass that tickled the taut skin on their bellies. The pace was slow, but time schedules were not a primary concern.

As far as the eye could see, not a man-made object marred the view. A gentle south breeze rustled the tall grass, causing a ripple on this vast, green prairie not unlike the waves on an ocean. To complete the comparison, the canvas cover of his little wagon might have been the billowing sail of a lone ship dwarfed by the limitless expanse of the sea.

It was a day and place to promise adventure. This was the land of the Indian, the Cherokee Outlet. Twenty years earlier it was the grazing ground for countless thousands of buffalo, which fed and clothed the Indians. More recently it was the range for Texas cattle. Over the horizon to the west great herds were at that very moment moving up the Chisholm Trail to the railroad yards in Kansas, for shipment to eastern markets.

The haze of the Indian summer day shortened his vision, but as he bounced along in his little wagon the curtain parted, and the wooded banks of the Chikaskia River came into view. A wisp of smoke beyond the trees suggested human habitation, and he guided his mules in that direction. It might be an Indian camp or it might be headquarters for one of the many ranchers who grazed herds on this land. It proved to be a ranch headquarters, the Three-K, owned by Ross Stratton. A lifelong friendship developed from that first meeting, and Prettyman was to name one of his sons for this rancher friend.

Delightful days in the out-of-doors followed. Game was plentiful, and since it was roundup time a photographer with Prettyman's creativeness had to hurry to keep up with the challenging and changing scenes on the open range. Unfortunately, only a few of the views he made have survived. Prettyman took his turn in the saddle, along with the seasoned cowboys, and made up for his deficiencies at the end of a lariat with his generosity in giving prints to new friends. The black nights were his darkroom, and the sun prints he made the following day could be developed in a curtained corner of the bunk house.

Around the campfires in the evening he heard the tales of men who had driven herds up the western trails, encountering en route all known varieties of weather, men, and Indians. These men, who enjoyed a freedom known by few but envied by many, extended a warm friendship to the young photographer. Ten years later some were to be with Prettyman when he entered the land rush of 1893. One was to turn outlaw when the demand for cowboys declined, but the change of professions did not end the friendship. As a farewell gift, the outlaw presented Prettyman with a worn copy of Dante's *Inferno*, proving, perhaps, that highwaymen in that era counted literary taste no professional handicap.

The days and nights went all too fast. A flock of wild geese winging southward reminded the visitor it was time to get back to his gallery to care for the usual pre-Christmas rush. A group of horsemen escorted Prettyman a short distance back across the now frost-bitten prairie, and during the final farewell of many revolver shots the mules took their bits in their teeth and ran like frightened deer. Some of Prettyman's choice plates were broken in the runaway.

During the next ten years Prettyman made at least one annual trip into the Indian country. Each year his journeys extended into more distant areas, and his time away from the gallery increased. Usually he went alone, but now and then friends accompanied him part of the way for a hunt, then caught rides back to Kansas on freighter wagons. His associates operated the gallery, and if the trip was to be long, his devoted wife took the three young sons on an extended visit with her relatives.

On the short trips, he photographed the strange bark houses of the Kaws and the mud lodges of the Pawnees, which some historians say were not built in the new land. Washunga, the great Kaw chief, was a willing subject, and a casual photograph Prettyman made of another aged Kaw warrior was later to be considered one of the greatest and most eloquent Indian photographs ever made. Eagle Chief and Baptiste Bayhylle, both of whom were in Major North's band of Pawnees during the Sioux outbreaks, were Prettyman subjects.

When Bayhylle posed for Prettyman he was both old and ill, without the strength or willingness to dress in the fine robes he possessed. He got up from his sick bed, wrapped a blanket about him, put on a high hat, and stood for an instantaneous exposure. Prettyman knew he had pictured one of the outstanding members of the Pawnee tribe, but with his usual indifference to the historical importance of his work, he labeled the picture only as "The oldest Indian in the Pawnee tribe."

In 1885, while making pictures among the Ponca Indians, Prettyman received a strange request. Some of these Indians, who lived only a few miles south of the Kansas line, had been taken by their agent to Arkansas City, and had posed for studio pictures. They treasured prints of themselves standing before painted backgrounds of trees, waterfalls, and rocks. Prettyman tried unsuccessfully to convince them they had better scenery all around them. They wanted waterfalls and rocks, not the trees and tipis they saw every day.

He went back to his gallery and had painted a selection of backgrounds which he rolled around tent poles and added to his load. They irked him, but when such backgrounds were demanded he draped them down the side of his wagon and placed the subject before them.

In the late spring of 1886 he planned a six-month tour of the Indian country. He put his family on a train bound for the home of relatives and set out at once to explore land he had not visited before. He went alone, for no close friend could find legitimate excuse to be away from home and business for such a long time. This time he took the Traders' Trail southwest into the reservation of the Poncas. He visited White Eagle for a day but made no pictures. He decided to see what new scenes were ahead before using his supply of plates, which could not be replenished without a return trip to Arkansas City.

In sign language, interspersed by words of warning spoken in the Ponca tongue, the rain maker of the tribe urged Prettyman to delay his journey the following morning. Even a tenderfoot could see the Indian was right, and Prettyman was no greenhorn on the subject of prairie storms. As Prettyman harnessed his mules, the old man kept up an incessant chatter while he tugged at the traveler's arm, and even attempted to remove the harness.

A general concern gripped the Ponca camp. Women scurried

about collecting the many objects that clutter an Indian village in mild seasons. Frightened children clung to their mothers as they darted in and out of the tipis, depositing their loads. Old men gathered in groups, chattering to each other and occasionally pointing toward the rolling clouds in the southwest, blackened even more by the rising sun. The young men saw to the horses tethered within the camp area. Even the numerous dogs added to the confusion with their whining and barking as they sought shelter in this and that lodge, only to be driven out by a scolding Indian woman with a stick in her hand.

Prettyman had to take a chance with the storm, he thought, to get across the Salt Fork of the Arkansas River before the promised deluge made a torrent of the now fordable stream. As he whipped his unwilling mules forward, he turned to wave at the old medicine man, just as a gust of wind caught the latter's soiled white robe and tore it from his body. It was an ominous warning.

Two ruts in the prairie guided Prettyman to the ford in the river, which he crossed without difficulty. A few miles over the ridge was the Otoe Reservation, which could offer shelter from the pending storm. Between him and that destination was nothing but prairie grass. He had not proceeded far along his course before the storm engulfed him in all its fury, and the incredible stories he had heard cowboys tell of tempests on the plains seemed gross understatements.

Every lightning flash made the mules try to jump through their collars, and the instantaneous cracks of thunder sent them back against the doubletree. Something had to give, and it did. The doubletree broke at the clevis pin just as the wind ripped the canvas cover off the wagon. Sensing their freedom, the mules lurched forward, and Prettyman reacted too slowly to avoid being pulled from the seat and hurled to the ground. He let go his strong grip on the lines and released the mules to dash wildly into the storm.

He made a futile effort to protect his plates from the rain by covering them with the painted backgrounds. His camera, guns, and ammunition had a lower priority in the emergency. He could not even find protection for himself under the wagon, since the howling wind bounced it about too much for safety. He lay on his stomach for

15

what seemed like hours, holding tightly to the tall grass while the rain poured and the wind screamed. Never again would he doubt the wisdom of an Indian.

Eventually the storm abated, and his first salvage operation was to fashion a new doubletree from a tent pole in the wagon. It might last until he could get back to the Salt Fork, where he could make a more durable one out of a hackberry limb. The mules were nowhere in sight, but since they were coupled together by the neck yoke only one search would do for both. Near sundown he spotted them, after walking for miles in a big circle around the wagon. There was no choice but to spend an uncomfortable night on the prairie, hungry, wet, and cold.

The following day he started back to Arkansas City. Although the Salt Fork was high, he managed to ford it without trouble. He was not anxious to meet the Ponca medicine man in his sorry condition, so he took a long way home. Back in Kansas, he repaired the damage to his equipment and, three days later, was on his way south once more.

From many sources he had heard of a band of unfriendly Indians who lived south of the Cimarron River in the same primitive state which characterized their ancestors in the Great Lakes region when first seen by white explorers. They were the Sacs, who constructed their dwellings and council houses out of bark from trees. Descendants of Keokuk were still leaders in the tribe, but the most belligerent chief was Pa She Pa Ho. He even refused to talk with the agent, so the story went, and he wanted no white man for a friend.

Prettyman made further inquiry about these people among the Otoes, who verified as best they could all the unfavorable reports about the Sacs. The Otoes had not visited the Sacs, since all tribes then were confined to the limits of their own reservations. However, Johnny Pipestem told Prettyman he could learn much about these Indians if he went first to the Iowas, whose land adjoined that of the Sacs on the west. The Iowas were friendly to the Otoes, and once when they lived in the north they were brothers.

Grazing cattle appeared more plentiful on the Otoe range than on any of the areas he had crossed. At noon he stopped at a side camp beside a stream where two cowboys were having their meal. He accepted their invitation to join them and found them well informed on the land and its inhabitants. The cattle, Prettyman was told, had just arrived from the south, as a result of a new lease made with the Otoes, and since they were on unfamiliar ground they grazed in bunches.

The cowboys knew the Sacs, one of them having worked the previous season on the Whistler Ranch, and found their Indian neighbors unfriendly. Prettyman was told to go southeast to a point where he would strike a wagon road that would lead him to the Iowa Reservation. This was the main supply route for agency goods, and the military road to Camp Russell, north of the Cimarron. Captain William L. Couch and his band of Boomers had traveled this road two years earlier in an unsuccessful attempt to colonize the Stillwater Valley. The trek was known as the "last raid of the Boomers."

Prettyman drove his mules hard that afternoon, but it was not until the following day that he found the wagon trail. Thereafter the journey was much easier. Washington Irving had called this the Cross Timbers. A heavy growth of trees lined the several streams, and even the upland was sparsely covered with squat oak and blackjack. It was a hunter's paradise. Wild turkey, quail, and squirrels seemed indifferent to his presence.

On the fourth day out of Arkansas City, he saw the Cimarron River. It was at swimming stage, which left no choice but to make camp and wait until the water receded. The thought was not unendurable to a sportsman. He backhauled to a clear stream that suggested spring water, curried and tethered his mules, and pitched his tent in a grove of towering walnut trees. His housekeeping duties completed, he set out to enjoy the obvious hunting opportunities that surrounded him. He was not disappointed. The river crossing could wait. It is surprising how hungry a hunter can get, and how savory is the taste of game birds cooked on an open fire before the blood has cooled.

Two sleeps later, as he prepared a particularly pleasing breakfast of fried quail, hot biscuits, preserves, and coffee, he was startled to see a tall Indian standing near by, almost close enough to touch.

17

Later, as he recounted his experiences, he said his first thought was of the hostile Sacs, and that he should attack this silent intruder with his hunting knife. He arose to face his adversary, and the Indian spoke to him in Etonian English. He was an educated Iowa, but only his speech revealed it. He had heard gunfire from across the river and, Indian like, had swum the Cimarron to investigate.

There was enough food for two, and as the Indian ate and dried his clothes, Prettyman explained his mission. The water was too high to attempt a crossing now, but the Indian said he would return later with oxen and some boys from the village, who would help get the wagon safely across the river. True to his word, the Indian was back on the third day and Prettyman was installed in the Iowa village. The oddity of the crossing experience caused him to set up his camera and show the Indian how to press the rubber bulb that tripped the shutter. Prettyman wanted to be in this picture.

He found the Iowas industrious and friendly. Although they hunted and fished to provide part of their food supply, he observed fields much larger than the squaw patches of the Poncas and Kaws, and freshly turned earth showed preparation for spring planting. He was questioned at length about the Indians he had visited, and he asked questions in turn about their eastern neighbors, the Sacs. They were not brothers, he was told. However, Chief Tohee believed he could go among the Sacs without inviting danger if he were the proper type of white man. The chief offered to send a runner to Moses Keokuk and ask him to be a friend of his friend.

After a brief and pleasant stay with the Iowas Prettyman moved on, to the east. The land was rough and wooded, with no traveled road between the two tribes to indicate friendly intercourse. Obviously the Sacs were not trying to be neighborly. He came at last within sight of an Indian village with a scattering of dome-like huts. There were signs of life, but if the approaching traveler had been observed, he received no recognition. He stopped his wagon in plain view, got down and walked around to the heads of his mules, then pretended to adjust their bridles, merely to show that his hands were empty and that he came in peace. Curiosity eventually would bring some young bucks out of the village.

He had not long to wait. Young boys came first, stopping a safe distance from the wagon. Older men joined the boys, and all came forward for a close look at the strange white man. One asked if he were the picture man who had just visited the Iowas. Chief Tohee was as good as his word about sending a runner. All wanted to see how the picture machine worked. Obviously Prettyman was the first photographer to visit them. A demonstration was promised, but at the moment he wanted to make camp. He was directed to a suitable site near a clear stream, within view of the village. Too many inquisitive hands forced him to ask for help in protecting his camera and plates. A sharp word from one of the adults ended the danger.

These Indians were different from any he had visited. The scantily-clad men were huge and muscular. Only a few wore their hair long, which seemed to mark them for special tribal assignments. Men of warrior age were close cropped, even closer than the Osages. Only a small tuft of hair, no more than an inch long, remained on the tops of their heads. Particularly noticeable was the respect shown the authority of leaders. The chiefs ruled as of old. Experience had taught him that few Indians were quick to reveal their knowledge of the English language, but he was to learn that this tribe did not want to speak like white men, and few understood his words.

Although he was the only white man in that village, he felt no danger. He behaved as he did in the many lonely camps he had enjoyed in the past, waiting for the Indians to make the first overtures of neighborliness. He hunted alone, prepared and ate his meals alone, and waited. Curious Indian children stared at him from behind trees, daring to come closer only when accompanied by an adult. Prettyman knew he was observed when he hunted, and he also knew his prowess with a gun could impress even the Sac warriors, one hundred of whom once defeated a thousand Indian enemies in a duel of guns and courage.

One morning four warriors joined him on a hunt. He was their equal in the forest, and excelled them in marksmanship. They enjoyed a meal together in the woods, eating as they had hunted, in silence. When they returned to the village one of his hunting companions indicated he would like to have his picture made. Other pictures followed other hunts, and a worn footpath appeared between Indian village and photographer's camp. Finally a chieftain invited Prettyman to the village; patience had broken the barrier.

Pa She Pa Ho greeted him coolly, but civilly. He had seen some of the prints of the warriors, and was curious about the process. In time he, too, agreed to pose, standing in front of his lodge, wrapped in his best Hudson's Bay blanket, his ancient otterskin cap covering his scalp lock. The weather was too warm for such attire, but the chief wanted all his finery. He was delighted with the results.

He wanted a group picture of every full-blood in his tribe, eighty-six of them, posed before the council house. He would permit no mixed-blood members in this picture, although they outnumbered the pure-bloods. Such was his attitude toward the whites. The one-hundred-and-seven-year-old mother of the chief was given the most prominent place in the picture.

"This is one of the most interesting pictures in my collection," Prettyman notes in one of his catalogs. Obviously he was influenced in his rating of it because it represented an important achievement, and not because of its technical qualities. The subjects could not be well arranged, possibly because of lack of co-operation, with the further difficulty of the language barrier. Some sat in deep shade while others were in bright sun, creating an uneven illumination that makes good reproduction impossible.

He made many pictures of these Indians, their lodges, and council house. Unfortunately, his plates of the descendants of Keokuk did not survive. The days went all too fast for him. Wild game seemed inexhaustible, and there were willing companions for every hunt. The shaded streams were inviting to an ardent fisherman, but the Sacs would not share this sport nor eat the results.

Some days, he loaded his wagon for trips into the unknown. The Indians were reluctant to see him go, and to placate them he left his tent, to make them know he would return. During his absence nothing at his camp was ever tampered with or stolen. He visited the Whistler Ranch at the request of the cowboy friend he met on the trail, pictured herds of grazing cattle, and spent a few nights with a group of cowboys who had a cabin in the woods. It was their hunting outpost.

By his reckoning he had been gone from Arkansas City almost six months. His family was due back soon, and he should be there when his wife and sons returned. He told the chief he must depart in two or three more sleeps and take his tent with him. That evening the tribal orator visited his camp to tell him he was to witness the sacred ritual of the Otter Skin Lodge. It was the highest honor the tribe could bestow on any white man. Much as he would have liked, he could not photograph any of the rites, even if there had been sufficient illumination to permit it.

The rites began with a great feast, and were to continue four days. The Indians already had completed the fasting portion and the ordeal of the sweat lodge. He sat cross-legged near the bubbling pots and enjoyed luscious portions of meat. He believed it to be venison. It was very late when he returned to camp, impressed by the devout attitude of a savage people toward their traditions. The next day he was told the "venison" was dog meat.

On the return journey he had no stomach for meat, nor did he allow meat of any kind to be served in his home until long after Christmas. A few years later an eastern artist visited the Sacs to make portraits of the Keokuk brothers. Prettyman had cleared the way for the artist's favorable reception, but Pa She Pa Ho never consented to sit for the painter. He preferred the picture he already had, of himself in his blanket, which he kept hanging on the wall beside his shield and peace pipe.

It is unfortunate that Prettyman kept no journal of his tours of the Indian country. Only those incidents that impressed him enough to tell, and impressed his hearers enough to remember, are preserved. He was a good story teller, but much of the flavor is lost in the retelling, and the many missing links in his narrative cannot be reconstructed. The little regard he showed for his precious plates indicates the lack of importance he attached to his adventures.

It is known that Prettyman spent some time among the Five Civilized Tribes in eastern Oklahoma, that he made pictures of the Cheyennes, Arapahoes, Comanches, and Apaches in the west, that he toured the land of the Shawnees and Potawatomis, but much of what occurred on these trips is unknown. Where the trips fit in the sequence of his Oklahoma career can only be guessed.

Sturdy remnants of once great tribes lured Prettyman to the northeastern corner of present Oklahoma, where a photographer had to work hard for a picture. Here in the foothills of the Ozarks were no endless stretches of prairie that could be navigated by lowering an occasional drift fence, or fording a placid stream. Some busy thoroughfares scarred the rolling land. A railroad went all the way through the Five Nations and crossed the Red River into Texas, but Prettyman was not one to follow a beaten path. Other photographers were doing that every day.

He went first along the Kansas border, east to Coffeyville. In this important border town photographic supplies could be purchased, if needed. He could have stayed in a comfortable hotel, stabled his mules in a wagon yard, and made day-long trips into the Indian country. That was the usual procedure, but it did not appeal to this man who had wandered over the western plains alone, with everything he needed in his wagon, with never a concern about the services of a doctor or the help of a companion in an emergency.

Across the border to the south was the land of the Quapaws, hemmed into the corner of the Indian Territory by the Neosho River. This was a land with a different atmosphere; the topography, the climate, even the people seemed of a different world, yet the ethnologists said they were Indians. They lived in permanent dwellings, wore citizen's clothes, and all seemed to have albums stuffed with photographs. By comparison with some of the western tribes he had visited, these were industrious people and well along on the "white man's road." They did not seem to him like Indians, without blankets, without peace pipes, and without the colorful skin and bead work worn by western Indians. They did not command his interest.

He noted little change in scenery and people as he moved south into the land of the Modocs, the Wyandottes, and Senecas. Intermarriage was more obvious, and he made a picture of a mixed-blood family that he included in his personal album of unusual pictures. He did not bother to identify it. He went on to the Cherokee capital at Tahlequah before he decided to return to Kansas. The roads were not to his liking. Every interesting side road he took ended abruptly at an Indian cabin. He went back to Arkansas City over the military road from Fort Gibson that went all the way.

It is little wonder that he was discouraged by the primeval fastness of this region. While the eastern part of the Territory contained thousands of acres of choice land, tilled principally by white tenants, and had many large ranches, it was a mountainous country. Old and established towns grew and prospered, built primarily by white people, who lived there only on permit and by payment of an annual head tax to the Indians. The land upon which these towns developed could not be owned by the whites, who had no system of levying taxes to support schools for their children, or to maintain local government. Laws of sorts were administered by tribal courts and by United States marshals operating out of the federal court of Judge Isaac C. Parker, of Fort Smith, Arkansas.

This kindly old gentleman earned the sobriquet of "Hanging Judge," since he had to resort to stern measures to quell the carnage that flourished under such conditions. He had a certain civil jurisdiction also over a large part of the Territory and made important decisions on land titles and rights of conflicting cultures with few legal precedents to guide him. The Sans Bois mountains were the hideout for outcasts of the world, and the Indians were powerless to prevent their crimes. Indian courts were for Indians only. Judge Parker sentenced 78 criminals to hang, but robberies, murders, and arson continued unabated until after the Territory became a part of the state of Oklahoma in 1907.

Conditions were such that in 1893 Governor Fishback of Arkansas sent a protest to President Cleveland. "I have good reason to suspect," he wrote, "that a very large percentage of the bank and train robberies which take place between the Allegheny and Rocky mountains are organized and originated in the Indian Territory. The federal jail at Fort Smith is at all seasons nearly full of prisoners from this territory, and the federal court holds sessions continuously through nearly every month of the year. This state of semi-chaos and the farces of government which exist in this territory suggest the time has arrived for the federal government to assert its right of eminent domain over it."

Prettyman went back into the area again before he ceased making periodic jaunts into the Territory. It must be surmised that he rode the train this time to visit the land of the Choctaws in the southeastern section. Faded pictures, but no plates, exist to show that he made a personal inspection of the beautiful country in the Kiamichi region. The Creek and Seminole nations were more accessible and closer to his base of operations. Much of the great Chickasaw Nation was, geographically, a southern extension of the western plains, which he visited before and after the country was opened to white settlement.

Where his next journey fits can only be guessed, but it is believed to have been in 1888. This time he went down the left bank of the Arkansas River, along the Agency Trail to the Osage and Pawnee countries. It was easy to get lost in the vast expanse of the Osage Hills. It still is. Prettyman was hopelessly lost for days. He traveled every day and made camp at night in places he had never before been. He saw no one, and never crossed a man-made trail, not even his own. Water and wild game were plentiful, and he wanted for nothing but a fix on his position. It is irritating to a wise and experienced traveler to be lost.

He knew he could find his way back to Kansas by the sun and stars, but he was there on a mission that had not been accomplished. Finally he surrendered to confusion and pointed his mules north for the Kansas line. A day of travel on a straight line brought him to the edge of an Osage village. Even though he did not know these people, he was pleased to see them. Unfortunately, the feeling was not mutual.

Everywhere he went he faced a sullen stare, or eyes without expression. His questions went unanswered, and no words were needed to tell him he was not wanted in the village. He did not know that a band of white men had stolen many of their ponies, and that the Indian police were after them at that very moment. Later, when told of the raid of horse thieves, he was grateful the Indian police had not found him alone in the hills. It is likely he would not have been heard from again. Guilty or innocent, a lone white man would have suffered from the wrong done the tribe by the thieves.

Although never overbearing or offensive, Prettyman went about the village seeking a friendly face, or a person who would consent to speak the words of a white man and tell him where to find the Agency Road. He saw one blanketed Indian who looked familiar and tried to speak with him. The Indian ignored him. Finally it dawned on Prettyman that he had photographed this man in his Arkansas City gallery. Then the Osage was wearing citizen's clothes, and was on his way back to the reservation after being graduated from an eastern college. He had an excellent command of the English language.

Prettyman challenged him with this information, and the Indian consented to speak. He remembered Prettyman and knew he could not be a spy of the horse thieves. He told the white man why he had been given the silent stare treatment and told others of the tribe who he was. Some of Prettyman's best Osage pictures were made during that visit.

Literally buried in the eastern end of the Cherokee Outlet was a "forgotten" tract of land that was to be prominent in Territorial history, but Prettyman knew it as the best hunting ground in the Territory, and the home of J. W. "Cherokee" Jordon, a life-long friend. Known as the "Triangle" because of shape, this area of 105,000 acres lay between the Arkansas and Cimarron rivers, their confluence forming the apex, and the Pawnee Reservation the base. Washington Irving mentioned it in his *A Tour on the Prairies,* following his visit in 1832. His description, in part, was:

"We were in a region of adventure, breaking our way through a country hitherto untrodden by white man, excepting perchance some solitary trapper. But all was silent, lifeless, without a human habitation, and apparently without a human inhabitant. It was as if a ban hung over this fair but fated region. The very Indians dared not abide here, but made it a mere scene of perilous enterprise, to hunt for a few days and then away."

Jordon, a one-eighth Cherokee Indian, had built a log cabin home inside the Triangle in 1883. Although it was held under the jurisdiction of the Cooweescooee District of the Cherokee Nation as unorganized territory, it could not be reached without crossing the Osage Reservation to the north, the Creek Nation on the south, or the Pawnee Reservation on the west. Armed with several commissions from the Cherokee Nation to govern this land, Jordon was virtually a king without subjects, except the wild animals of the forest, in this small domain. Because of its isolation, it became a hideout for criminals, and outlaws and marshals played hide and seek in the Triangle for twenty years.

When the Boomers hunted a loophole in the law that might permit occupation of some portion of the Indian Territory, they concluded that the Cherokee Outlet no longer belonged to the Indians, since the latter had abandoned it. Once, when the buffalo roamed the prairie, the Cherokees needed this outlet to journey across the plains to the buffalo areas east of the Rocky Mountains. When white hunters destroyed the buffalo, the Indians no longer used this broad avenue for its original purpose, and Boomer lawyers believed Indian title to it had been extinguished. If that were the case, they argued, the Outlet automatically reverted back to the government and became public domain, subject to homestead settlement.

Judge Parker of the Fort Smith court knew the law better than the Boomer attorneys. He also knew about that trim log cabin deep in the woods of the Triangle. When he umpired the argument he pointed out that the Outlet had not been abandoned, since Jordon lived in that area, and that the ranchers who grazed cattle there paid rental to the Cherokees for the right, and therefore were agents for the Indians.

Boomer resentment at this court decision resulted in attacks on Jordon and efforts to drive him from the Triangle. Jordon built a tower-like fortress behind his cabin resembling the stockades that dotted the frontier in earlier days, and from behind its protective walls fought off every Boomer assault. Prettyman preserved this unique private fort in his album of interesting pictures.

Ed Hewens and Milt Bennett established the Bar X Bar Ranch in the Triangle in 1884, then grazed more than fifteen thousand head of cattle on its lush meadows. Like Jordon, they lived with a situation they could not change, and expected frequent visitors out of the shadows who gave no names and kept their sojourns short. Hewins and Bennett observed the code of the range that kept all doors unlocked, tobacco on the mantel, and food in the pantry. These were for use by needy persons who were to molest nothing else.

"We had an understanding in the Triangle," Jordon said, "that no crime was to be committed here, and that men on the scout who sought safety here were to find no foe among us." Members of the notorious Dalton gang once dared to borrow some horses from Jordon's herd to replace some spent ones they had ridden while fleeing from a posse. Jordon sent word that if the horses were not returned he would join the posse. The missing horses appeared immediately, with a substantial cash rental payment tied to the mane of one.

Over the years Prettyman was a frequent visitor at the Jordon home, and the Prettyman home in Arkansas City was a second home to the entire Jordon family. The Triangle was a hunter's paradise, and when Prettyman loaded his wagon at Arkansas City he would tell his family he was going to the "happy hunting ground."

Prettyman had never known Arkansas City without Boomer camps around its fringes. Some Boomers had waited along the border since 1879, always hopeful that next year some portion of the Territory would be opened for settlement. He had pictured these people around their wagons and campfires, his camera revealing their privation and suffering. It would appear from their pictures that the thousands of acres of good land in the settled western states, available for homestead, would have been a better choice for them, but they preferred to wait for land in the Territory, or starve if necessary. They eked out meagre existence by performing day labor when they could get it from the farmers of southern Kansas. Boomers came and went, but each year their numbers seemed to increase.

Early in 1889 legislative deliberations ended the wait. In March the world knew that one portion of the Territory, the Unassigned Lands, in almost the exact center, would be opened for settlement the following month. It was to be a type of opening never before seen in American history, and people came from all nations to participate in it. Contenders for this land were to line up outside its borders, and at a signal at high noon, April 22, they were to race and scramble for what they could get. It was to be expected that such a promise of excitement would attract all sorts of people, which was precisely what happened.

As the great day neared, people in the Boomer camps outnumbered the permanent residents of Arkansas City. It was a photographer's dream, and Prettyman kept busy. He was not one to stay in a darkroom, however overloaded he might be with work, when there was drama to be photographed. Never was such a kaleidoscopic thing staged for a photographer. Harried women herded their broods in the crowded zone around the family wagon which was larder, bedroom, and dressing room. A campfire on the ground was the kitchen.

Men hunted wood and water for family use, traded horses, or consulted maps in secret, like gold seekers, which were supposed to show location of the best claims. The maps may have been bought from a faker for a needed dollar, but few buyers had seen the promised land, and most could not detect a swindle. Gamblers with tired, dull eyes wandered through the disorderly mass of vehicles, seeking men who might have a few dollars to risk on a "sure thing." Prospects were scarce. Men washed red undershirts in dirty, sudsless water, and some obvious tenderfeet tried to make friends with strange horses they hoped to ride to the best quarter section obtainable. At night musical instruments were brought out of wagons, and families who were strangers two days earlier joined in popular songs of the day. Frequently religious hymns were drowned out by near-by groups singing bawdy bar-room songs.

Every known profession, honorable and otherwise, every state and territory were represented here. Prettyman could (and did) record an amazing chapter in history here in the groves along the Arkansas River.

Four days before the opening, the Boomers were allowed to cross the fifty-eight mile Cherokee Outlet and take positions around the land to be opened. Arkansas City became a deserted village, a large part of its permanent population joining the Boomer ranks at the last minute. Prettyman was one of these.

Trains were running into the Promised Land, and a person could be a pioneer on a green plush cushion in a day coach, but Prettyman preferred his wagon. The journey south was duly photographed. One unusual incident required several plates.

When the first wagons reached the Salt Fork, the river was at flood stage. Captain Jack Hayes of the Fifth Cavalry had charge of the procession, and the responsibility of getting more than four thousand laden wagons, and many times that many people, to the starting line before noon on April 22. The river appeared to be rising. It would have been foolhardy to attempt to get even one wagon across the torrent. Hayes obtained permission to lay a heavy flooring of lumber over the rails on a railroad bridge that spanned the river. Lumber was brought out on a special train and the wagons were rolled across without mishap. The officer's charges reached the starting line in time.

When the signal sounded a mad scramble began. Fewer than one-fifth of these frenzied land hunters could hope to be successful, since there was not enough land for all. The beautiful prairie became a junk yard of broken vehicles and blasted hopes. Prettyman went on to Guthrie, the predicted metropolis of the Territory. He was one of a few to picture the birth of a city, to capture fleeting scenes when a bare prairie became a gathering of twenty thousand inhabitants before the sun set.

Here was drama, but it is unlikely that Prettyman or any of the thousands of other tired and dirty participants were aware of the importance of the occasion. The cities and towns of his youth were born before the days of photography. Only the west offered natal scenes of cities to photographers, and only the Territory south of Kansas provided such amazing labor pains that could be photographed.

Since he did not come hunting land, Prettyman had time to find unusual scenes to shoot. He photographed the things that interested or amused, and time has proved his judgment good. His picture story of Guthrie is a book in itself. He found some Arkansas City friends secure on a lot, and he made his home with them.

His camera recorded Charles W. Constantine, the former mayor of Springfield, Ohio, as he called the crowd around the wagon from which he spoke on the morning of April 23, urging government by consent until such times as laws could be enacted. He photographed the first election, the only one of its kind in recorded history, when men in two lines walked past a wagon containing counters, each line representing the supporters of each of the two candidates for mayor. His camera could not show the men who walked past the counters, then ran back to get in line and be counted again. This odd method of stuffing the ballot box nullified that first election try.

He stayed a long time in Guthrie, finding a ready sale for his views. He recorded the replacement of tents by crude buildings, the clearing of streets of claimants who had settled there, and a variety of early homes. Later he produced an album which showed his best of Guthrie's settlement. He found time to visit Oklahoma Station, later known as Oklahoma City, and Kingfisher, Edmond, and Norman. Even after he returned to Arkansas City he made frequent trips back by train to add more interesting pictures.

Never again was he to give a new town such coverage, but he was to be a part of every other run and opening to take place in Oklahoma. In 1891 he jumped the Cimarron River to photograph the race into the Iowa and Sac and Fox country. He lost his equipment in the river and came back without a picture. In 1892 he raced into the Cheyenne and Arapahoe country and found it dull compared with the first opening. He was ready now to set the stage for one of the greatest historical pictures ever made.

The Cherokee Outlet was scheduled for opening on September 16, 1893. His frequent exposures to the "run" disease had made him a Boomer. This time he was going to be a contender for land; he already had selected a quarter section he wanted. It was to be a nineteen mile race, but he knew the way better than other contenders.

Always a photographer, Prettyman worked the waiting line for days before the opening. It was the same old story; men and women on horses, in wagons, on foot, on bicycles, all with dirty faces and all with hope in their eyes. Fringed surries drawn by spirited horses were waiting beside ancient wagons powered by ox teams. Newspapers said this was to be the greatest of all the openings, but viewed through the ground glass of his camera, Prettyman could see little that differed from the other three.

The only real difference to him was the heat and dust that choked and killed. It had been an unusually dry summer, but the mid-September heat added to the discomfort. As he worked up and down a line that seemed a thousand miles long, he could rarely be sure he had a picture because of the thick fog of dust. If only he could find some way to relieve the monotony and take a picture that was different.

Dust! A refreshing idea came to him out of all that miserable, sifting sand. He would build a platform that would place his camera above it, and from that vantage point he could photograph more of the line. He hurried back to Arkansas City and ordered two wagon loads of lumber to be dumped just inside the fence on the Chilocco Indian School ground, which was at the extreme east end of the line. Before he went home the night before the race, he made sure the lumber was there.

Cowboy friends from the Three-K ranch were at his home when he arrived the evening before the race. They wanted to ride with him the next day, just for the fun of it. They had uncomplimentary words for homesteaders and nesters of all descriptions, but if Prettyman wanted to be one of those people, they would help him all they could. As they packed their saddle bags, Prettyman told them of his plans for a picture of the race.

He hired four carpenters to meet him at the west corner of the Chilocco farm at sunrise the next morning. They were on time and soon had an odd-shaped tower protruding into the air. Jokes were frequent and varied about this construction job, but Prettyman avoided the site as much as possible to keep his secret. Less than an hour remained before starting time when the job was completed. He drove a wagon alongside and handed up three cameras. Then the reason for the high platform was obvious.

Photographers came in droves, representatives from the metropolitan newspapers of the East and professionals who wanted good views to sell. They pleaded for places on the platform, and some waved bills of large denomination to emphasize their requests. Money could not sway Prettyman. Three of his associates manned the cameras as he hastily gave instructions for each to try to guess the proper fraction of a second when the shutter should be tripped. There could be no retakes.

His picture plans completed, he joined the cowboy friends who held a place in the line for him. Looking back, it was a strange decision for a photographer to make, and stranger still that one like Prettyman should make it. No claim in the entire Outlet was worth as much as an unusual plate of this drama that would take place just once. Prettyman was unable to answer this question when asked of him later. The only reasonable answer is that the race offered excitement, and that was more than money to him.

A soldier's carbine and a bugle call set the impatient line in motion, and four men on good cow ponies were among the first to leave. Unlike most runners, these men knew where they wanted to go and lost no time getting on course. The grinding roar of shouting men, galloping horses, and rolling wagons was all behind them. The crowd thinned as they raced. These four experienced horsemen knew how to handle their mounts, carefully chosen for this important race, and the first half hour was an exciting thrill for them all. Suddenly Prettyman's horse stumbled, his foot in a prairie-dog hole.

He was thrown from his saddle but neither horse nor rider were hurt. At that instant, and for the rest of his life, Prettyman was grateful for the presence of his cowboy friends. Two of them pocketed his horse, a difficult maneuver in that wild stampede. The third rider stood by, risking his own life to protect that of his friend who would have been trampled to death if he had been left alone on the ground. It would be suicide to stand still in that mob, its force exceeding that of any other wild stampede that had taken place on this same prairie in former days. They were back in the race in less than two minutes, according to their later reckoning. One hour after they left the starting line, all four were on the desired quarter section. It was good time in any race.

The light camera he had strapped to his saddle bag was not damaged in the accident. Prettyman made a picture of the flag that marked the claim as his, and the faithful horse that brought him there. Then, leaving two of his friends to defend his rights, he and the third cowboy rode back to Arkansas City.

He had left instructions that no plates were to be developed until he returned, but his associates were too interested in the outcome to wait. The plates had been processed, and the most desirable one was blistered by temperature indifference. Some hot words passed in the dark room that day. An examination of the plates showed one photographer had made a fortunate choice, and exposed his plate just as the line broke. This picture became world famous. Demand for prints taxed their facilities and threatened to burn up the plate with too frequent use. A glass positive was made and additional negatives made from this positive. Prettyman ruled that each should have a negative and that the picture was not to be copyrighted.

One of the photographers on the platform was afflicted with "buck" fever and made his exposure before the line was in motion. The third exposed his plate as the heavy vehicles lumbered across his view. It may be assumed that the three photographers exposed their plates at two-second intervals. The third picture in the series was considered too blurred by movement to be saleable. Demand of the time was for crisp sharpness, which was considered more important than the story-telling qualities of a picture. It remained unknown, gathering dust in a basement storeroom until it was recently given modern evaluation. It could become the greater picture of the two.

Fast film and fast shutters were unknown in 1893, and for movement to be frozen on a slow plate was a miracle in itself. Many other photographers were present that day, but all the rest made pictures before the line was in motion. Prettyman's foresight in having photographers work from a platform caused the pictures his associates made to be outstanding.

Prettyman waited in line for days at the Perry land office to file on his claim, then moved his family onto it to comply with the law, which required actual residence before new land could be owned. He built an uncomfortable house which neither he nor his family enjoyed. It was fortunate for posterity that Prettyman was not a farmer. While his neighbors broke sod for spring planting, dug wells, and otherwise prepared for a difficult winter, he went about in his wagon making pictures of pioneers struggling to exist. He was able to hire the necessary farm work done, employing grateful neighbors with teams and plows who had no outside income.

A town sprouted up from the prairies four miles to the north of his claim—a habit of towns those days. Every claim holder hoped his piece of land would become a site for a city and make him wealthy. Too many towns came into existence, some to attract no more than a wagon-load of groceries sold across the tail gate of a wagon. A few boasted a blacksmith shop, and fewer still had post offices operated from private dwellings. Prettyman watched this town to the north take shape. It was called Blackwell Rock at first, and finally just Blackwell.

Little persuasion was needed from the family to cause Prettyman to sell his claim and move to Blackwell. He sold his interests in Arkansas City and established permanent residence in the Territory, which had become more like home than any other part of his known world. The *Arkansas City Traveler* gave him a scathing editorial rebuke for taking his talents elsewhere. He built a two-story brick building, the first in Blackwell, for an "ultra modern" studio, reserving a large lounge for the display of his Indian views.

He was to serve Blackwell twice as mayor, headed the board of trade, assisted in establishing a college there, helped construct water and electrical plants, and had a large part in getting a railroad for the growing city. Such useful activities sound commonplace when associated with a man who had courted danger and adventure in primitive places among stone-age people. He made no more long trips, but photographed the last run in history, into the Kickapoo country east of Oklahoma City, in 1895, and was on hand with his camera during the milder openings when the last of the land that belonged to the southwestern tribes was made available to white settlement.

Prettyman was thirty-five years old when he opened his studio in Blackwell. He had been eminently successful and could look forward to continued prosperity. His was a name known far beyond municipal boundaries. The great and the unknown came long distances to sit before his camera. Frequently a grizzled cowboy or a dejected Indian came. Indian finery had disappeared, but Prettyman knew the secret yearning of these old friends and kept a special wardrobe which helped recapture the splendor of the past.

It would seem that a man could be happy with an enviable professional reputation, respectability, a fine family, a beautiful home, and an income that could provide luxury. A person given all the high offices and positions of trust a community offered should be content to live out his days in that place. Citizens in the new country had survived pioneer hardships; the prairie bloomed with fields of lush crops; fat cattle filled the pastures; and comfortable homes dotted the landscape. Blackwell shed its swaddling clothes and gave every promise of becoming an important city. A feeling of well-being was everywhere.

Prettyman made pictures of shocks of golden grain, of white farm homes in a beautiful setting of trees. He photographed trains unloading products of the factory and loading products of the farm. There was talk of the Territory's becoming the forty-sixth state. This was a land too far north for the drouth and heat; too far south for the biting blizzards. Crops of both the north and south grew here in the midlands. Nothing could prevent this fair land from fulfilling its destiny of greatness.

Prettyman lingered longer and longer each passing year in his exhibition room lined with pictures of the old west. He would gaze for an hour at the picture of Pa She Pa Ho wrapped in his Hudson Bay blanket, or at "Cherokee" Jordon sitting on the rail fence around his log home. Sometimes he stayed too long in front of his pictures while impatient customers paced the floor of the waiting room in his studio.

Something was missing; something he sought and could not find in the jingle of the cash register, not even in making the best pictures a photographer could produce. He did not share his thoughts at the time, for he could not put his finger on the trouble. If Jim Bridger had been there he could have explained; or Kit Carson, or Old Bill Williams. They all tried to leave the free life of the great open spaces, but came back after a fling at civilized living. But they could still lose themselves again in the untamed wilds when they decided the easy life was not for them. Prettyman could not. It was gone.

Pa She Pa Ho was dead. A Territorial newspaper gave this account of his passing in 1898. "Robed in his otter-skin dressing and bear-claw necklace, with his tomahawk and gun, pipe, tobacco and his favorite photograph, he started on his journey to the happy hunting ground."

35

Dan Tohee was dead. A tribesman killed him with a garden hoe in 1903 during a dispute over who should care for the crops. The ways and implements of peace also could lead to destruction.

The Triangle now was a checkerboard of tilled acres, every infamous outlaw who had sought sanctuary there was dead, and the deer and elk that fattened on its succulent herbs had been served on the tables of hungry homesteaders.

He had to get out of Oklahoma Territory. The fields of tall corn made a pretty picture, but not for him. He saw the virgin prairie crowded out by corn. He saw herds of fat cattle grazing where game had once been plentiful. Clumsy wagons rolled on dusty roads where Indian ponies had trotted through the soft grasses. A white school building was the centerpiece of a yard of shouting children where once the cowboys of the Three-K Ranch had their cabin home. He, too, must go.

He sold his prosperous business, his home, and moved to the Far West in 1905. Just as he abandoned his priceless plates in his Arkansas City gallery, he left behind all his Blackwell collection. Not even the beautiful prints that lined the walls of his salon were to go. One camera went with him. It had been in his wagon on many prairie tours, and the one that made the great picture of the land rush of 1893. He sold it to a used camera dealer shortly after his arrival in California. One of the greatest of all professionals had turned his back on photography for good, leaving fires and indifference to wipe out the bulk of his contribution to history.

The remaining twenty-five years of his life can be covered in a few lines. He established a wholesale drug business in partnership with his son, Ray. It was too confining and he turned it over to his son to operate while he developed an orange grove. His wife died in 1916, and he was buried beside her in 1932.

Destiny could not have chosen a more dedicated photographer, schooled him better for an understanding of the position of the Indian, the cattleman, the Boomer, and the homesteader in their contentions for possession of the by-passed Territory, then placed him in the most suitable geographic position to record a dramatic epoch in history. He photographed virtually every important actor, borrowed none of their bitterness, and could be called friend by them all. Soldiers and marshals who policed the Territory, Indians, agents and missionaries, cattlemen, and every Boomer leader were photographic subjects and close acquaintances.

"He photographed many Indians who never before had consented to have their pictures taken," according to Ray, his son. "After his first four years of visiting the reservation there was hardly a day when you would not see Indians and cowboys in his gallery. He was the first photographer ever allowed to make pictures of the Ponca Sun Dance and the Squaw Dance. His trips into the Territory were always exciting and sometimes dangerous. Once he nearly drowned while crossing the Cimarron River."

His son's personal description rounds out the man. "He was of medium height and weight; quite good looking. He was a determined man who sought and enjoyed adventure above everything else. Hunting was his favorite sport, but he excelled in them all. He did not have much of a formal education, but was a great reader. Money was never his foremost ambition. He enjoyed discussions, and had some strong opinions about history, religion, and politics, but what I always admired in him was his gracious admission of defeat when he found he probably was wrong."

It never occurred to Prettyman to detail all his adventures, or that his experiences were historically significant. Not until he approached his death bed was he made to realize that generations still unborn deserved to know of his life on the frontier, the people and events it had been his privilege to know. He agreed then to dictate his story, but paralysis stilled his voice before he began. Now only his eloquent pictures can speak for him, and tell with many irritating interruptions the fusion of the races.

Largely to one man goes the credit for preserving what little is left of the thousands of plates made with such precision and perseverance. He was George B. Cornish, a protégé and youthful partner of Prettyman's who had a greater respect than his teacher for this monumental record. Cornish stood on the platform that hot September day in 1893 when one of history's greatest photographs was made. He manned one of the cameras and tried to guess the fraction of a second when a fast-moving scene would reach its dramatic peak. He never revealed which of the three pictures was his.

Cornish continued as a photographer in Arkansas City throughout his life. Each time he moved to larger quarters he took along the remnants of the work of both Prettyman and Bonsall. To assure their continued existence he made glass positives of many of these plates, which he kept in careful storage. Only when an original negative was broken did he open the store to make another negative. When unbreakable acetate film became available he made negatives on this material.

Never did Cornish attempt to borrow the greatness of his teacher, nor claim the authorship of his work. Some he protected by copyright in his own name, but these pictures continued to be identified as Prettyman's work. Prettyman never sought a copyright on any of his pictures. Long after Prettyman left Kansas, Cornish produced an album of photographs made from choice plates in his collection. He did not have to include his former partner's name but he titled the album "Oklahoma Views, by Prettyman and Cornish." After the death of Cornish, the plates became a part of the Cunningham Collection, and now are back in the land of their origin.

2. Prettyman Learns His Trade

WHY WILLIAM S. PRETTYMAN decided to become a photographer is conjectural. In the densely populated East, the land of his birth, photographers were numerous after the Civil War, and it is likely he could have had a choice of opportunities to become an apprentice in this profession had he been so inclined.

He preferred life in the out-of-doors. When he had completed a common school education, he entered construction work. Hunting, fishing, and outdoor sports consumed his spare time. There is no record of his showing even a casual interest in what was to become his life's work until he came West, where photographers were scarce and apprenticeships virtually impossible.

When he arrived in Kansas in 1879, he found a ready market for his skill as a builder, but within a few months he became manager and then owner of a roller skating rink, a popular and profitable occupation at the time. His scrapbook reveals that he was successful as a rink operator, but it does not record why he exchanged the status of proprietor for the confining and low-paying job of darkroom attendant in an unpretentious gallery in a community where there was little money to be spent on pictures.

Photography was beginning to shed its swaddling clothes when he first experienced the uncomfortable closeness of the mysterious little room at the back of the gallery. A smoking kerosene lamp, shielded by a ruby glass window, illuminated but faintly a row of shallow wooden trays. There was no ventilation, and the odor of the smoking lamp combined with a smell of acid to cause anyone who loved the out-of-doors to question the advantages of photography as a profession.

Collodion plates were still in use on the frontier in 1880, although they had been almost completely replaced by dry plates in the cities of the East. One of the many tasks of an apprentice was to strip and clean glass, to be recoated and used by the photographer. Another job was to carry three buckets of water from the well outside and pour them gently over the plates after they had been exposed, developed, and fixed.

Printing of the plates was done by sunlight, a job that could be learned quickly after the apprentice had developed a respect for the fragility of glass plates. Developing, washing, and toning of prints also were tasks easily mastered, but carding was an operation that caused many apprentices to change professions. Each print had to be glued securely, without bubbles or wrinkles, and perfectly aligned on a backing of heavy cardboard. These cardboard backs were expensive. Most photographers had their names embossed in gold lettering on the lower margins, and some had additional advertising printed on the backs. To spoil one by gluing on a "squint" picture meant a reprimand, and to ruin two meant dismissal. An apprentice had to be careful.

Prettyman worked his way through the chores entrusted to the unskilled, always a perfectionist, until he was ready to take his place behind the camera. Here was a challenge of both hand and mental skills, the manipulation of both man and material. The adjustment of the curtain across the skylight to illuminate the subject required judgment, as did the choice of exposure, but a good or bad photographer was identified according to the way he recorded his subject. The time was past when any likeness was a good likeness. Prettyman became a good photographer whose talent was discussed in Wichita and Kansas City, and as far away as St. Louis.

When he opened his own gallery, men and women came from all these distant places to sit before his camera. During the ten years he was in business in Arkansas City, scores of people of importance in the Southwest sat for a picture by Prettyman, and most of the men who won places in the history of that section became his friends.

The gold-embossed lettering on the rigid backing of his pictures was to change from time to time. Once it read "Prettyman and McFarland." Later it was "Prettyman and Miller," and the last partnership was "Prettyman and Cornish." These and others were the men who operated the gallery when Prettyman took prolonged tours into the Indian country, south of Kansas, to photograph an era soon to disappear.

I. H. Bonsall, a Civil War photographer of more than ordinary ability, went out to Arkansas City after the great conflict had ended, bringing with him a number of his favorite views, including this one of his gallery taken shortly after the death of Abraham Lincoln in 1865. He was to be William F. Prettyman's teacher.

Summit Street, Arkansas City, photographed by I. H. Bonsall in 1873, half a dozen years before Prettyman arrived to take up his profession as picture-maker.

The Arkansas City that young Prettyman saw in 1879 on his arrival
in the West. Before him was the first gathering of the Boomers at-
tempting settlement of the Indian Territory.

Prettyman's mentor, Bonsall, like all Civil War photographers, needed at least one plate of the Great Emancipator. Here was inspiration for an eager youngster.

An old Civil War veteran still in his blues was the kind of subject to challenge Bonsall as well as his aspiring apprentice. Bonsall had captured the spirit of an aging G.I. of the War of the Rebellion.

Cheesecake from the frontier:
an early example of Prettyman's work.

During his first year in Arkansas City, Prettyman was confronted with the increasingly dramatic surge of frontiersmen eager for a stake in the Indian Territory. Here he caught a group of Boomer leaders, posed in front of "one of the best hotels."

William S. Prettyman as Bonsall photographed him shortly after he started his work as an apprentice. A headstand held him steady for the twelve seconds needed to expose the glass plate.

On his own as a photographer, Prettyman was quick to seize adventure by the forelock. Here he is about to cross the Cimarron River in Indian Territory with a vehicle of his own design, which became known from the Kansas Border to Texas and from Arkansas to Colorado.

3. Indians in the Territory

"SOUTH OF Arkansas City there is such a sudden transition from richness to poverty, from civilization to barbarism that it is difficult to comprehend what the quick landscape change means. A group of Indians, lazily moving along the road on their patient ponies, explains the transformation. You are in a territory that belongs to our brother in red, who is always behindhand. The Kansas border is an imaginary line separating something from nothing; dividing modern civilization from bluestem solitude."

This quotation from a widely circulated piece of "Boomer literature" sums up the sentiment of the people of the West in the 1880's. It was a time when Indian depredations were fresh in people's memories, when the westward migration was at its height, and when land owned by the Indians seemed greener and more fertile because it was beyond the grasp of white men.

It was obvious, even to the disinterested, that the Indian Territory could not continue in its present state for many more years, solemn treaties to the contrary notwithstanding. Canvas covered wagons containing settlers, their families, and belongings, crowded the streets of Arkansas City, and countless campfires illuminated the groves along the Arkansas River at night. Here was a mighty army, poised on the border of the forbidden land—the Promised Land—that was not to be denied forever the right to enter and possess.

In the gateway city optimism ebbed and surged in the Boomer ranks. On some days, the opening of a part of the Territory reached the "any minute now" stage, and Prettyman wondered if he would be in time to make a photographic journey into the Indian country before its inhabitants would be engulfed by white civilization. A month, a year, a decade might be granted him to make the final picture record of the Indian in his primitive state.

Some changes already had taken place among the Plains Indians, because of the influence of agency schools and missionaries, but a photographer could still find manners and customs very much like those that the Lewis and Clark party saw eighty years earlier. He could even find a few aged Indians who remembered this expedition. The older Indians clung to the ways they knew best, resenting and resisting attempts to interest them in a new culture. Schools, new religion, and strange medical practices were not for them.

Their children were caught between the two cultures, existing in a confused state of contradictory teaching. It was only through them that progress could come, the agents and missionaries contended. Schools were established to educate the Indian children, and were maintained through the difficult and discouraging years following the Civil War. Children had to be removed from their family circles to boarding schools, away from the influence of their parents, before they became receptive to instructions alien to their ancient ways.

In the eastern half of the Indian Territory a different situation existed. Indians of the Five Civilized Tribes and the lesser groups located adjacent to them had the advantage of more than half a century of education and association with the white race. More whites than Indians lived in the eastern portion of the Territory, and although assimilation was far from complete, ancient Indian customs virtually were forgotten.

Although blood was to be shed during minor clashes between the two civilizations in the future, Prettyman gave no thought to his own safety as he bounced along in his wagon over the vast plains of the Territory. With the passing of years his wagon became known, and he frequently was stopped by a lone rider who invited him to come to his village. Indians went out of their way to make him welcome.

Prettyman lived off the land, and when he hunted for food he would be gone from his camp hours at a time. His property was not molested, but he frequently returned, laden with wild game, to find a party of Indians sitting beside his wagon waiting for an invitation to supper. Fresh meat was available almost without effort, and the

Indians regularly availed themselves of nature's bounty, but they could not make soda biscuits like those the photographer baked in a dutch oven buried in a mound of hot embers.

An appetizer usually was requested by the guests before meals, but the Indians soon learned the picture man neither carried nor consumed firewater, much to their regret.

Prettyman's early association with the Indians was to prove advantageous later. When treaty groups came into the Territory to persuade or force the Indians to take land as individuals rather than as tribes, relations between the races deteriorated to the point of bloodshed. All surplus land was purchased by the government, and later occupied by white settlers.

When the Indians were forced into individual ownership of family-sized tracts, they gave up tribal government, self-determination, and many of their ancient rituals and traditions. This was an important step toward citizenship and progress along the white man's road.

None of the bitterness the Indians held for the white race was directed at the photographer. He was always welcome, and when he ceased to visit them they sought him out in his gallery at Arkansas City. Even the embittered chief of the Sacs, Pa She Pa Ho, who stood on a hill near his village in April, 1891, and watched white settlers spread out over his beautiful land, arranged a special feast for Prettyman, who came with the settlers, but for a different purpose.

Prettyman was intensely interested in wild Indians. Here he pictures perhaps the wildest. These Apache women exhibit the hostility of a proud, fierce people towards an encroaching civilization.

Beef issue on the hoof. The Comanches, when Prettyman went among them in the mid-eighteen eighties, a short decade after their devastating raids had been stopped, could be seen slaughtering their beef allowance on the spot. Man seated is consuming it "hot."

Cheyenne police, photographed about 1884, helped the United States Army keep order among their kinsmen in Indian Territory and drive out white intruders—land seekers, whisky runners, horse thieves—prevalent upon the last frontier.

When Prettyman established a difficult friendship with Pa She Pa Ho, chief of the Sacs, he took this invaluable photograph of a leader who lived in the past and wanted nothing the whites had to offer. He wears a Hudson Bay blanket, an ancient otterskin crown, a bear-claw necklace, and Great Lakes type moccasins. He carries a peace pipe fashioned above a tomahawk.

Wacomo, the Sac and Fox orator at the time Prettyman visited these tribes. Among his people his eloquence was said to be almost the equal of Tecumseh, the brilliant leader of the Shawnees. His long hair marked him as being outside the warrior group and is unusual among his kind.

Prettyman found at the Sac and Fox village about 1885 the same type of bark house that Lewis and Clark had encountered when they first visited these Indians in 1805. Third from left is Pa She Pa Ho, the Sac chief.

Sitting Bull, the famous Sioux, poses for Prettyman in a studio setting not in keeping with his attire. This is one of the few Indian pictures by Prettyman not directly related to the Indian Territory.

Gall, a leader of the Sioux in the battle of the Little Big Horn, strips to his fighting attire to pose for Prettyman. When this photo and the one of Sitting Bull were made, these and photos of General George Armstrong Custer, whom the Indians had annihilated in 1876, were in greater demand than photos of Abraham Lincoln.

Prettyman identifies this picture only as "a Tonkawa Indian," a member of the last and smallest tribe to arrive in the Indian Territory. His people, preyed upon by other Indian tribes, whose hostility to the Tonkawas was intense, had finally to appeal to the federal government for help. The census of 1900 showed only fifty-nine Tonkawas, most of whom were past middle age.

The Indian Territory was a veritable paradise for the student of aboriginal inhabitants of North America. David Tohee of the Iowas headed the most peaceful band of Indians not listed among the Five Civilized Tribes. He is pictured before a canvas tipi in 1885.

When a man could afford two wives (or more), he took them. This Comanche medicine man is shown with his women against the backdrop of a prairie village.

Prettyman calls these "Cheyenne Indians very scantily dressed" in his catalog compiled in the late eighteen eighties. Clearly they are dancers, some of the finest human specimens among the warriors of the Old West.

Government agents were already stationed among the Plains tribes when Prettyman got into Indian Territory. One of their most perplexing problems occurred when an entire tribe abandoned livestock and growing crops for an extended stay with Indians some miles distant. Here the Iowas move out for a visit with their Otoe cousins. Leading horseman carries a single scalp of a battle long past.

Washunga, chief of the Kaw or Kansa Indians, lived only a short distance south of Prettyman's gallery in Arkansas City. To many Americans he looked "the way an Indian should."

When he took this picture of a Kaw bark house, Prettyman preserved for history an architectural type fast disappearing even in his time. It is similar in shape to the earth mounds of the Pawnees and Mandans, and the bark houses of the Sacs.

A Kiowa boy in Indian-made clothing shows the influence of the uniforms of white soldiers—probably of Fort Sill—upon his people. The pin stripe on the side of his trousers is strictly army. The layers of necklaces are the additions of a fond mother.

Kiowa girls model their best raiment for Prettyman's camera. The taste of these Plains women tended more towards fringe than towards the ribbon work of neighboring tribes in the western half of the Indian Territory.

Betty Falls, a Kickapoo woman with her baby, captured on a glass plate before 1890 by Prettyman on one of his trips into central Indian Territory.

"The Royal Family" of the Osages, all bands—Great Osage, Little Osage, Black Dog, and Arkansas—exhibiting everything from long hair to the more typical roaches, were photographed in Prettyman's studio in Arkansas City about 1887. Che To Pa is second from left in the middle row. He held about four hundred of the best Osage warriors on the Federal side during the Civil War.

For this prominent Osage, Gray Horse, an Indian village still in existence was named. He has in his left hand a copy of the tribal roll, in his right hand are two eagle feathers, and his braids are encased in the classic beaver skin of nineteenth-century warriors.

▶

▲

Prettyman tells the story of meeting the seated Osage in his studio on the latter's return from Haskell Indian Institute at Lawrence, Kansas. A short time later he encountered him in the Osage country in Indian Territory, where he had happily resumed the dress, customs, and language of his people.

▶

A studio portrait made by Prettyman of two Osage women. Note striped blanket-shawls, still to be seen today among members of this tribe, who are now centered in Pawhuska, Oklahoma.

An Osage dance team shown on their reservation about 1885. As early as the last quarter of the eighteenth century, the Osages had intermarried with French traders and trappers, so that by the time this picture was taken mixed-blood characteristics are noticeable and many tribesmen expressed themselves as well in French as in Osage.

Having once broken through the barrier of Indian reserve, Prettyman found willing subjects among all the tribes. His son said, "I can't recall a day when there were not several Indians around my father's Arkansas City studio." Here Ma To Pak of the Otoes is pictured with his family.

Medicine Horse, a prominent chief of the Otoes of northern Indian Territory, posed for this portrait in 1883. He is garbed as his forebears might have been, with a magnificent bear-claw necklace, his ears weighted down with brass rings, and around his neck a sea-shell necklace for good measure.

In the center of this group is Barnaba, the Ponca-Omaha interpreter for the Otoes, with Wa Tha Ka Tha Ga, left, and La Neway, right, of the Otoe tribe. La Neway was known as Little Pipe and was also photographed by one of Prettyman's contemporaries, William H. Jackson, during the latter's trip to the West with the Hayden Survey.

By 1887 the attempt was being made by many tribesmen, exemplified here by a group of Osages, to leave the wickiup in favor of the frame dwelling introduced by the white man. Prettyman's picture is the story of this transition, snapped on a wind-swept March day.

Prettyman found humans, white or red, much alike in their fondness for children. This young Otoe, Wayne Headon, poses with miniature instruments of ancient Indian warfare.

Pawnees continued the ancient method of curing hides even after the buffalo were gone from Indian Territory. This is a cowhide being readied for moccasins and other leather-work. George Bird Grinnell, the famous ethnographer of the Cheyennes, once used this photograph.

These Pawnees are pictured on tour with Pawnee Bill's Wild West
Show about 1890. Prettyman's photograph was made when the two
Bills, Pawnee and Buffalo, had competing shows on the road.

Baptiste Bayhylle, an interpreter and scout for the Pawnees during
the Sioux wars, was also photographed by William H. Jackson and
D. F. Barry. He was almost 100 years old when this picture was made
by Prettyman in 1885.

Eagle Chief, a Pawnee leader who participated in the Sioux Wars and was a subject for every prominent photographer of the period.

Examples of the winter and summer homes of the Pawnees in the eighteen eighties. The earth lodge, of ancient development, was used for the cold months, the summer house was a tipi with its covering (here canvas) rolled back to catch the breeze.

War Chief of the Pawnees, so named, in the center poses with William Pollock, left, and Ralph Weeks, right. Pollock was the first Indian artist to follow Renaissance styles in painting. He later rode with Theodore Roosevelt's Rough Riders, and was decorated for bravery in the Spanish American War.

The Poncas prepare for the Sun Dance about 1883. Left, barely discernible, is the medicine bundle. Each candidate is painted for the dance and carries a feathered spear in his mouth.

Like a modern-day carnival scene, this tableau of one phase of the ritual of the Sun Dance by the Poncas offers a sight never to be recaptured. Prettyman caught it before it was discouraged and finally banned by the federal government.

In 1890 when the Ghost Dance craze was at its height in Indian Territory, Prettyman made a distant photograph of a Ponca village and
then superimposed a photo of a herd of buffalo in the foreground.
The Indian messiah had said that the buffalo would reappear, the
white man would disappear, and the land would belong to the Indian
once more.

Displaced persons are the same everywhere—harassed, resentful, perplexed. These Poncas are shown with their temporary abode in the
Cherokee Outlet in 1887. Back of their brush arbor is a cattleman's
drift fence, the first if not the most permanent evidence of settlement.

Plural marriage among the Poncas, 1887: left, Red Leaf and four wives; right, Stands Yellow and three wives. By this time buffalo hides for lodge coverings were already rare. The coverings in this small village were of canvas.

Above-ground burials were common—almost the rule—among the tribes of the Indian Territory. This is a Ponca graveyard photographed in 1884 by Prettyman.

While the Poncas were no friends of the Sioux, nevertheless they borrowed some of the dress characteristic of their enemies on the Plains. The Poncas were great movers—nomads in the real sense of the word. They were settled with the Quapaws in northeastern Indian Territory, but their discontent caused the government to relocate them in part of the Cherokee Outlet purchased from the Cherokees.

These Potawatomi girls are members of one of the largest tribes of western Indians. They were quick to adjust to new conditions after they were removed from Kansas to the Indian Territory.

Prettyman probably would have chosen as the best of his pictures this one of all of the full-blood members of a Sac village. Pa She Pa Ho, the chief, stands front center in white summer robe. In front of him, seated in the place of honor, is his mother, then (in 1884) 107 years old. She remembered the arrival of Lewis and Clark in the northern villages of the Sacs almost eighty years before.

4. Era of the Cattleman

THE FIRST HERD of Texas longhorns that swam the Red River and moved north without invitation into the Indian domain created a fabulous industry, as well as a romantic era in western history. At first the Texas ranchers wanted to use the Indian Territory only as a highway to market, since it was the one practical avenue open to them. They had beef to sell which overflowed their ranches during the Civil War, at a time when the East was hungry for meat.

Land of hostile Indians lay between the ranches and railroads, but possible high profits offset the hazards of the journey. Longhorns by the thousands followed the first small herd that went up the trail in 1866. A few dollars, a few beeves, and a few bottles bought consent from the Indians. A few more negotiables changed hands and the ranchers moved in for a long stay.

The highway became breeding and grazing ground, months closer to the railroads. The lush grass that once supported countless thousands of buffalo now supported countless thousands of cattle. Lease payments, not always on schedule, made the arrangements acceptable. Western Indians, although less familiar with barter and balance sheets, had adopted a revenue raising plan the more advanced eastern tribes employed successfully. For years the Five Civilized Tribes had rented their grazing land and admitted whites into their country at so much a head.

Branding pens, drift fences, even ranch headquarters buildings appeared, constructed along crude architectural lines dictated by the frontier. Scarcely anywhere else in North America were such ideal ranching conditions available, and at such a low price. Water and grass were plentiful, and winters were mild enough to permit herds to live on the open range, surviving on the dry grass until early spring greened the prairies.

This bonanza attracted investors from all parts of the world, some to speculate as silent partners, while others, who wanted the glamor and excitement of range life, invested their time as well as their money. English peers and European barons adjusted themselves to cowboy saddles and joined forces with the sons of American bankers, railroad men, and politicians. This new type of outdoor living caught the fancy of the world, and the cowboy, perhaps the most romantic figure in American history, was created on the rolling prairies of the Indian Territory.

After the eastern palate had been satiated by several million head of longhorns, consumers began to complain of the stringiness of the meat. Ranchers were responsive to demand and bred up their herds with cattle that could hardly survive a trail drive, but dressed out better in slaughter houses. Now that Indian land near the railroads could be had for a song, cattle did not have to be as muscular and long-legged as they did when they had to walk from Texas to Kansas, swim all the rivers in between, survive all the storms, and yet be in relatively good condition on native grass by the time they reached the railheads.

Ranching in the Territory settled down to become substantial business. In the north, a group of men formed a powerful association to deal with the Indians, the government, and any other group or individuals that concerned them. Known as the Cherokee Strip Livestock Association, with every rancher in the Cherokee Outlet a member, this organization was powerful enough to offer to buy the entire Outlet from the Cherokees at a price higher than the government offered when homesteaders first threatened to overrun the land. The government refused to approve the sale.

Numerous ranches existed outside the Outlet, wherever good grazing land and water were available, but in most other instances ranch owners dealt for lease and grazing rights as individuals.

Within the Indian Territory was one tract of almost two million acres of choice land the ranchers could not lease. It was known as the Unassigned Land, over which no tribe had jurisdiction. The government had control of this land but chose not to lease it. This anomaly was to lead to the destruction of the cattle empire as well as the Indian domain.

Ranchers fought hard to retain their rights to graze Indian land, and the Indians supported their cause. Regular grass payments from tenant ranchers were preferred to complete loss of their land, the anticipated result when reservations might be opened to white settlement.

As one reservation after another was opened to settlement, ranchers were required to remove their herds on relatively short notice. For a time it was possible to move cattle from a reservation that had been opened to one that had not, but shortly after the turn of the century the last of the grass land was overrun by settlers, and the heyday of the great cattle domain was no more. A few ranchers lost great fortunes when they had to give up grazing rights and dump their cattle on an unfavorable market, but while grazing lasted the prairies of Indian Territory produced a formidable tide of wealth.

The day of the cattleman in the Indian Territory was relatively brief—
just about twenty years, from the beginning of the cattle drives from
Texas after the Civil War to the first settlement in 1889. Here are two
typical cowboys, nameless but resolute, as their side arms indicate,
photographed by Prettyman in 1885.

Men "with the bark on" were as photogenic in the Indian Territory as in Texas during the same period. Erwin Smith, who came a little later, would have found common photographic ground with Prettyman, as this photograph shows.

Watering and cooling a herd in the Salt Fork River about 1887. This is part of the Ross Stratton spread often visited by Prettyman during the decade after he had learned his trade.

The Turkey Creek Ranch west of present Enid, Oklahoma, showing perfectly composed, unposed cowboys at dinner. In the whole repertory of cowboy photographs, there is scarcely another that surpasses this one, made when "the dew was on the grass" in the American West.

Roundup time meant hard work in all weather for all hands. In the countless miles of rich prairie land of the Cherokee Outlet, one could encounter scenes such as this, taken before white settlement had occurred and before the federal government had moved for land in severalty for the Indians.

A huge ranch in its time, with many hands, was administered in the
Outlet from a modest cabin such as this, pictured under construction
about 1883.

These primitive cabins were the only homes the Indian Territory cowboys knew. Here they spent their infrequent off-duty hours, with banjo and harmonica for musical accompaniment to their songs.

When ranching was temporarily stopped in the Cherokee Outlet, some cowboys preferred to make a living with a six-shooter rather than a plow. Here is Prettyman's photograph of Dick Yeager, a good cowboy turned outlaw. When the Cherokee Outlet was opened to white settlement in 1893, Yeager made the race with Prettyman "just for the ride." He gave Prettyman his copy of Dante's *Inferno,* thereby proving himself no stranger to letters.

In November, 1896, Dynamite Dick and Ben Cravens, two notable outlaw riders of the Cherokee Outlet, fought a battle with peace officers north of Blackwell. An hour later, Prettyman re-created the scene of battle and made this photograph.

Dynamite Dick, the outlaw, posed without protest for this last picture. His missing fingers, lost in a gun battle at Ingalls in 1893, made
his identification easy. He had been a member of the Doolin gang,
and was "killed" more times than any other outlaw of his time, as
reward-hungry possemen attempted to give his name to many an un-
identified body.

These horses were ridden to the scene of battle by the two outlaws, but members of the posse led them away. Cravens was severely wounded in the fight but survived and escaped to add further crimes to his already impressive record.

The Hunter: Deputy United States Marshal Cheeseman poses for Prettyman as he moves up the outlaw trail in the Cherokee Outlet. He apparently favored the cross-armed draw, judging from the position of his six-shooter.

The area in northeastern Indian Territory known as the Triangle was an anomaly. Unclaimed, it offered 105,000 acres of grazing land, which J. W. "Cherokee" Jordon put to use, with Ed Hewens and Milt Bennett, whose Bar X Bar Ranch carried 15,000 head. Prettyman photographed the Jordon blockhouse with two young defenders prepared to meet all comers.

The Triangle was a hunter's paradise. In front of the Barker Outlaw Cave are, from left to right, the Reverend A. C. Kronk, Arkansas City; J. W. "Cherokee" Jordon; and W. S. Prettyman himself.

5. The Boomers Gather

A RESTLESS population, uprooted and disturbed by the Civil War, fanned out to the West in search of new opportunities in frontier territory. Covered wagons rolled where trains did not run, carrying entire families with all their possessions, and depositing them as fancy dictated over the nation's vast possessions west of the Mississippi River.

For years the tide by-passed the land of the Indian and took claims in the new states that needed immigrants to continue development. Long before all the good land of Missouri, Kansas, Nebraska, and the Dakotas was settled, agitation began to force the opening of the Indian Territory to settlers. Militant leaders, such as David L. Payne, William L. Couch, and Milton W. Reynolds, espoused the cause of the settler, with strong seconding by the railroads.

Public opinion, long since aroused by mistreatment of the Indians of the West, posed a serious problem to the Boomers. Early in the campaign it became clear that the mere suggestion that the Indian must be dispossessed once more would doom the assault upon the Indian Territory to failure. The cattlemen became the adversaries of the Boomers, moreover, and allied themselves with the tribesmen.

In their contentions from press and platform, Boomer leaders made it clear that settlers wanted only equal rights with the cattlemen, who quickly became the villains in the plot. The first likely target for settlement was the Unassigned Land, in the center of the Territory, which could be taken without dispossession of Indians, since none lived in that area. It had been obtained from the Creek and Seminole Indians by treaty in 1866, to be used, it was hoped, to relocate nomadic tribes from the settled states. It was not used, however, for that purpose, which led to the designation of Unassigned Land. Its clouded title made it different from any other land in the Territory, and Boomer leaders exploited this difference.

They also extolled the virtues of this land of promise until the half-settled homesteaders in other sections were willing to abandon two or three years of hard labor for a new start in a land where success would come with less effort. Many families starving in dugouts on the bleak plains of the north, after two seasons of sod-busting and chinch bugs, loaded up and left for Arkansas City on being exposed to Boomer literature containing such statements as this:

"Products of the more northern and extreme southern regions will furnish the greatest yields in this warm soil and genial climate, free comparatively from the forces that dwarf their development in the Gulf states and lake regions, or the mountainous areas of New England. Climatically the conditions are perfect. Topographically the inspirations are not wanting. The atmosphere is electric and full of life-giving properties."

When Prettyman arrived in 1879, Arkansas City already had a sizeable Boomer population. It could be divided into two groups: those who wanted land, and those who wanted land in the Indian Territory. There could be no other classification, for they came from everywhere, were of all age groups, and of every known profession. Hope, determination, and poverty were common to them all.

Penetration of the forbidden land by a railroad in 1887 buoyed the hopes of all the Boomers who waited. Railroads, too, were opposed by the cattlemen, who were aware that civilization followed the rails and produced towns along the rights of way. The railroad ended the need for cattle drives, and it also hurried the end of the golden era of ranching in the Indian Territory. The Boomers now had a well-financed ally to help them in Washington.

For some of the patient people, it had been a ten-year wait. Many had to settle in other regions as the years piled up and their finances dwindled. Some went into No Man's Land, now the Panhandle of Oklahoma, where Indian rights did not exist, and helped to settle this area. Others took land in near-by states.

In the early spring of 1889, the wooded groves along the Arkansas River literally overflowed with Boomers. The date for the first opening, that of the Unassigned Land, was set for April 22. The long and discouraging battle with the ranchers had come to an end.

120

As the year 1889 dawned, it became clear that one of the greatest land rushes in history would shortly take place. Eager settlers from many parts of the United States were converging on the Indian Territory to await the opening of a small central portion of it known as the Oklahoma District or Unassigned Lands. Prettyman, sensing the epoch-making character of the event, followed it from the beginning with his camera. This photograph shows an encampment of those who would shortly make the run.

Photography was still too slow for candid shots, but Prettyman tried anyway, as here with the vanguard of the male aspirants to free land in the Territory. These are the faces of America's pioneers at a quiet breakfast a few days before the Run of 1889.

Courage and daring were essential qualities in the pioneer—with or without family. These youngsters and their parents were moving towards their destiny in a new land. When the run began on April 22, 1889, would they, or would they not, be among the lucky people who would get and hold a quarter section? Only one-third of those who made the run were successful.

As the fateful day approached, sources of drinking water became a problem for the waiting thousands. One enterprising future citizen had found and roofed over a spring and was selling drinking water by the pail.

For endless miles the covered wagons of the pioneers move up to the starting line for the land rush. Here the procession through the Cherokee Outlet is held up by the swollen Salt Fork River. At the extreme right, however, may be seen a railroad bridge.

Captain Jack Hayes, the escort officer on duty at this point, secured heavy timbers, laid them across the steel rails of the railroad bridge, and marshaled the able-bodied males for the arduous job of pushing and pulling thousands of heavy wagons across the stream.

The last hours before the Run of 1889 are being whiled away here.
The following day, on April 22, the great event was to take place.

Yesterday the prairie; today a city is born. This is the bustling scene caught by Prettyman's camera at precisely 4 o'clock in the afternoon on April 22, 1889, as the city of Guthrie emerged.

Prettyman's title for this one was "Holding a Town Lot," and in it are two of his Arkansas City friends, Peter Pearson, nearest the camera, and Dr. Aker, rear, who are in the act of becoming founding fathers of Guthrie.

By mid-afternoon on April 22, 1889, claimants of homesteads appeared in front of the land office at Guthrie to establish legal rights to their lands. Lot claimants were not eligible to file here; they simply had to fight it out for a few months.

Lawyers set up practice in the new land as quickly as they could drive a stake on a vacant plot of ground. These men "learned in the laws" are ready for business at Guthrie.

For many who made the run, news from home was hardly a second order of business. Here they await the arrival of a train with mail coming south through the Indian Territory to what had not even been a whistle stop before: Guthrie, again April 22, 1889.

Five days after the first town lots had been claimed at Guthrie, some twenty thousand people were busy creating permanent structures. In the distance are tents stretching to the horizon.

In May, 1889, Prettyman took this picture of Oklahoma City, now a metropolis of more than three hundred thousand. He was looking west on California Avenue.

At this spot, as Indians from the area near Guthrie and their agents posed for Prettyman, the first capitol of the future Oklahoma was to have been built. But it was not to be: Oklahoma City won the right to have the capitol twenty years later.

City building was not the be-all of the new Territory; country folk had quickly to get on with the business of raising crops. And clearly the age of oxen was not past, nor the primacy of horses and mules established.

Guthrie residents staged a special show for visiting congressmen, who had backed the Oklahoma Bill, when they made an official inspection on May 14, 1889. A group of Iowa Indians were brought to the busy town for local color and paraded between the rows of unfinished buildings.

6. Oklahoma Land Openings

Few of the milling thousands of Boomers around Arkansas City in the spring of 1889 knew or cared how they had won their battle with the ranchers. Nor does history record all of the machinations for the opening of the Unassigned Lands that went on in Washington during the final hours of President Cleveland's administration. But the main outlines are clear. First, the "Oklahoma bill" failed in the Senate, then reappeared attached as a rider to the Indian appropriations bill. This latter bill obviously had to pass if the administration of Indian affairs nationally was to continue. It passed and the Oklahoma provision rode to victory with it.

The time of opening was set at high noon, April 22, 1889, when the world was to have a new experience in land settlement. It was to be a race, with eleven thousand quarter sections of land as prizes for the fastest runners and nothing for the also-rans. Conservative estimates are that six to ten contenders for each quarter section participated in the race. More losers than winners crowded the border of the Unassigned Land on opening day.

Sensation hunters were not disappointed by the opening, for many complications were added to the simple race for free land. No provision, for example, had been made for the location of cities and towns, therefore none had been surveyed and platted. No municipal ordinances were proposed in advance, and no rules were established for organization of city governments. No courts existed to settle the differences between men. A few soldiers and marshals represented law and order, but they had no authority to name the victor in each individual race for land. Only the weapons in the holsters of settlers could enforce claims to the legitimacy of particular quarter-section holdings.

Thousands of "Sooners," men who stole in before the opening

and occupied choice land before the honest settlers could cover the distance from the starting line, added to the confusion.

Before nightfall on opening day, all the best quarter sections had from one to six claimants, but the most violent turmoil was reserved for the mushroom cities. Guthrie had the edge among contending towns, and an estimated twenty thousand persons congregated there on opening day. A Department of the Interior ruling permitted the use of only two quarter sections for a townsite. Settlers at Guthrie used four times the allotted amount before sunset, and four towns, with four sets of officials, divided only by a street, had to be formed.

Early the following morning a mass meeting was held at Guthrie and the settlers agreed they must have laws and live by them for the common good. The solution was government by consent, with courts irregularly established and enforcing "homemade" laws.

On the slope east of the depot, a disorganized mass created an unparalleled example of how democracy solves its problems. In rapid sequence, almost as if they were working from a prepared plan well rehearsed, Guthrie settlers held an election, appointed officials, surveyed the town, laid out streets, and fined gamblers for public funds until a tax base could be established. A similar pattern was followed at Oklahoma City, Kingfisher, and other territorial towns located at the time.

In the rural areas, first consideration had to be given to preparation of the soil for a first crop. It was almost too late in the season to plant, but only the soil could provide food for the families of the settlers. A shelter of sorts could come after the virgin sod had been broken and enough life-giving grain and vegetables planted to meet winter needs. Most rural families lived in wagons, or in tents if they had them, while seed beds were being prepared for crops.

It was a difficult first year for all who stayed. An abundance of wild game fed many families until the soil could produce. It was necessary for some men to leave their families behind on their claims while they sought work in neighboring states, to earn enough money or produce to maintain themselves on their holdings.

Not all had the courage or willingness to stay. The unsuccessful departed immediately, or became squatters by permission on the land of the more fortunate. Then there were rumors in the air of other openings, possibly better land, the kind described in earlier Boomer literature. Hundreds of good claims were abandoned as settlers sought the pot of gold in other areas.

The opening of the Iowa, Sac and Fox, and Potawatomi reservations in 1891, adjoining the Unassigned Land on the southeast, was a milder repetition of the first settlement. Only the arrangements for the opening were different. This was a settlement of occupied Indian land, and the Indians had to agree to take individual allotments, then sell all surplus land to the government, which in turn made it available to settlers. Identical conditions prevailed in the opening of the Cheyenne and Arapahoe reservation in 1892, adjoining the Unassigned Land on the west.

Two other openings by run were attempted, the Cherokee Outlet in 1893 and the Kickapoo Reservation in 1895. Undoubtedly the opening of the Cherokee Outlet was the greatest land rush of them all, since it covered more land area, and attracted more contestants than any of the others. It covered an area fifty-eight miles wide and more than one hundred miles long that ran along the southern border of Kansas and filled the vacant area between the settled areas of the Territory and the state of Kansas.

Other openings were by lottery and sale, while the great area occupied by the Five Civilized Tribes was added when statehood was granted to Oklahoma in 1907. All the Indians of the Five Tribes were required to take individual holdings, then the surplus was disposed of to individuals direct, rather than through the agency of the government. It took eighteen years for the entire territory to be settled by whites, for the Indians to be given the status of citizens, and for all to take the same road toward fusion of the races.

In all, there were five land rushes in the area embraced by the Indian Territory: the Oklahoma District or Unassigned Lands, 1889; the Iowa, Sac and Fox, and Potawatomi-Shawnee country, 1891; the Cheyenne and Arapahoe country, 1892; the Cherokee Outlet, 1893; and, finally, the lands of the Kickapoo, 1895. In the faintest morning light on April 19, 1892, Prettyman caught the assembling land rushers who that day would dash into Cheyenne and Arapahoe country. It is in every sense a historic picture.

At 7 o'clock in the morning of September 11, 1893, five days before the great run was to be made into the Cherokee Outlet, Prettyman photographed the long lines of prospective settlers registering near the south line close by Orlando.

On September 13, 1893, land seekers were still coming in to register for the Cherokee Outlet opening. Prettyman was everywhere making pictures. But for once he was caught in the act. He appears at the lower left in this picture, talking to a customer-settler.

One hundred thousand people joined the race into the Cherokee Outlet. These are some of them, their canvas-covered wagons stretching to the horizon in the upper left corner of the picture. It was taken on the Kansas line as the eager throng jockeyed for position.

In this and the succeeding two pictures we have history as it actually occurred. From a high platform he had erected especially for the purpose, Prettyman and his associates made one of the last possible shots before the race was to begin. In a few minutes he joined the race himself, leaving picture-taking to his associates.

At the starting signal at high noon, September 16, 1893, one of Prettyman's associates atop his platform squeezed the camera bulb and got this picture, one of history's most valued photographs, a landmark in "news photography" in its day and ours. Inset picks out of this dramatic onrush the balky horse, his rider's quirted hand across his chest ready to deliver a lash to the horse's right flank.

Two seconds later another photographer on the high platform snapped his shutter. The slower wagons have replaced the horses in this view. By standards of the day, it was considered too blurred for use; but today, the slow shutter timing gives understandable action and movement, virtues in themselves.

The horse, the claim, and the virgin prairie in the Cherokee Outlet, moments after the great race began. There was good grass as far as the eye could see, uncropped save by the buffalo herds of two decades before and the drifting Texas cattle that followed them. The claim is Prettyman's, as is also the horse.

The Cherokee Outlet was destined, in the main, for wheat culture, but the prairie sod first was broken by oxen, some of it being burned off in preparation for fall plowing. It was a soil blessed by calcium and phosphorus, rich beyond the imaginings of the pioneers.

The run into the Cherokee Outlet was made in earliest autumn, but on these plains the chill winds came soon after. Building materials were scarce—much of the country was treeless. "Soddies" constructed from chunks of prairie turf, partly below ground, partly above, were an obvious answer to the homesteader's need.

As the months passed, some of the "amenities" of settled life began to make their appearance—planks for wooden construction, a rough door, a stove, perhaps even curtains. This was no life for a lady, but by the thousands they survived it.

If a man had a shotgun, he could live well off these prairies while awaiting his first crops. If he had a dog, that was better still. Greater and lesser prairie chickens were present in great flocks, bobwhite quail were in every covert, and along streams there were deer and turkeys.

A year after the run, in 1894, more comfortable "full soddies" began to appear. This one even has windows, and the roof is of sheet metal.

Given a few years more, the new settler was able to construct a frame house and buy a fine new buggy. The grain shocks in the background bespeak prosperity from a rich soil—and hard work.

In less than half a dozen years the cow-pasture appearance of the Cherokee Outlet was gone and true affluence began to be evident. On land near the claim he had staked and sold, Prettyman made this picture of a bountiful harvest, with the home that wheat had built in the background. *The Oklahoma that Prettyman loved was no more!*

7. Fusion of the Races

INTERNAL STRIFE was predicted early in the nineteenth century when thousands of red men were moved into the Indian Territory to get them out of the settled states. Tribes had warred and preyed on each other since ancient times, and their concentration into a smaller area merely shortened the war trail, so reasoning went. A period of internecine wars did occur, but the plan of concentration was proved correct by time.

Tribes intermarried, customs were borrowed, and it soon became impossible to identify a tribe by articles of use. In 1885 the Pawnee agent was astounded to see Cheyennes join the Pawnees in their sacred dances. Here were two hereditary enemies dancing with the scalps of each others' relatives dangling from their coup sticks. Tribal visitations plagued and irritated the agents, who were then unaware that they would contribute to the final fusion of the tribes.

With the mellowing of fierce tribal and family pride came a better climate for the acceptance of a still more alien culture and a willingness to make adjustments with a bewildering world surrounding the Indian. Fusion of the races actually began with the first association of Indians and whites, to be accelerated by schools and continued association. As long as Indians were confined to reservations, agents could report little progress in attitudes and industry among many of the tribes, but with whites as neighbors and the forced abandonment of ancient systems of government, rapid progress began to be noted.

Although Indians of the Five Tribes maintained their government longer than the Indians of the West, they operated under constitutions and legislative systems that were modern and efficient. They maintained excellent schools, sent their leaders to the best colleges in America, and were the rivals of any race in intelligence and adaptability. Only a few proud full-bloods remained after a century of association with the whites.

Late in the eighteenth century, Dr. Samuel Johnson toured the Western Isles of Scotland and made recorded observations that might have been made a century and a half later in Indian Territory. He mentioned that when the wild tribes were broken up, and the power of the clan chieftains removed, the savage element that had been secure for centuries behind the impenetrable mountains became as other inhabitants of the British Isles.

As a photographer, Prettyman resented the civilizing process he observed in the Indian Territory. The pictures he could make in the land of the Five Tribes were not worth the difficult journey. He could make photographs almost identical with them in his gallery at Arkansas City. To him, Indians needed beads and blankets, tipis and savage dances, medicine men and the bloody trophies of war, if they were to be fit subjects for his camera. He could find none of these among the Cherokees or Quapaws.

During the latter journeys he made to the western Indians, he saw the same conditions developing and was aware that in a very short time these Indians, too, would assume the white man's ways, and eventually even the bronze in their faces would be bleached by a mingling of the blood of the two races.

It remained for an Indian to make the eloquent summary of the fusion of the races. He was the Honorable Wylie McIntosh, a Creek full-blood, whose life span had covered much of the period of transition of his people. He accepted the inevitable, as did the majority of thinking Indians, and put his views in these words:

"No one with judgment can predict anything but disaster for the attempt to preserve Indian autonomy. The time for its disappearance has come and it is now better for the Indian that it should disappear, and with it all that remains of his ancient customs and traditions. Their surroundings are such now that they could not possibly continue as they have been, even if both white and red desired it.

"The fact may be a sad one, but it is, nevertheless, a fact, that there is no longer a place on the soil of the Union for an Indian as an Indian. The pathos of his situation should and does appeal to all great men, but the logic of fate is not moved by the prayers of a fallen race, nor is their destiny averted by a tear for their end."

In eastern and southern Indian Territory settlement was hardly a new principle in Prettyman's time. Many tribes, removed there from the Deep South beginning as early as half a century before, had already enjoyed a large measure of "civilized" progress. The pattern of development had been set, and there had already been a large measure of white infiltration and intermarriage. Here is a Quapaw family and their dwelling at the time of the first runs.

This large ménage probably is a representative of one of the Five Civilized Tribes, although it is not identified in Prettyman's private album, where he kept his most interesting views.

Prettyman could not reconcile large-scale farming and livestock raising, permanent dwellings, and fences with Indian life. He therefore
spent little time with the Five Civilized Tribes, but here is another
of his views revealing the unmistakable southern influences upon
these tribes.

Joel Bryan Mayes, chief of the Cherokees, the most advanced of the
Five Civilized Tribes in Prettyman's travel years, shows how thor-
oughly these tribesmen had abandoned Indian clothes.

The long step towards the white man's road: Indian boys and their teachers at Sacred Heart Mission in the Shawnee country before the turn of the century.

And the final, dramatic end of an era: a survivor of another generation sits perplexed as he attempts to understand the proposals of the white Indian agent, just outside the picture, for his future. He too has abandoned Indian clothing for issue garments, which his women have fashioned to his style.

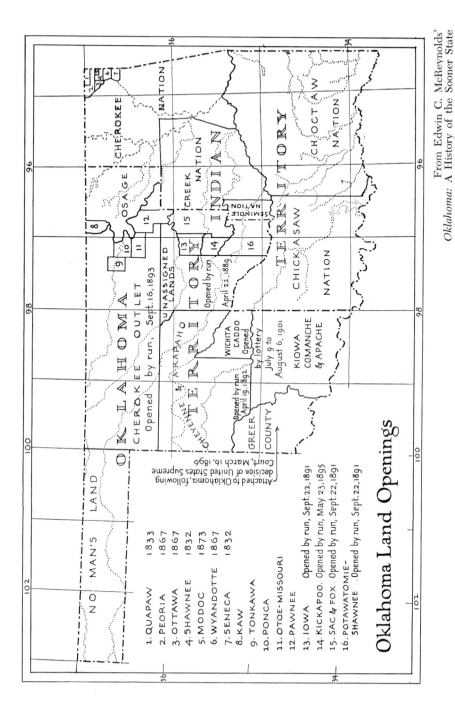

Oklahoma Land Openings

1. QUAPAW   1833
2. PEORIA   1867
3. OTTAWA   1867
4. SHAWNEE   1832
5. MODOC   1873
6. WYANDOTTE 1867
7. SENECA   1832
8. KAW
9. TONKAWA
10. PONCA
11. OTOE-MISSOURI
12. PAWNEE
13. IOWA   Opened by run, Sept. 22, 1891
14. KICKAPOO. Opened by run, May 23, 1895
15. SAC & FOX. Opened by run, Sept 22, 1891
16. POTAWATOMIE-
    SHAWNEE . Opened by run, Sept. 22, 1891

Location of the Indian Tribes and the Sequence of Land Openings
in Prettyman's Time in Indian Territory

From Edwin C. McReynolds'
Oklahoma: A History of the Sooner State

INDEX

UNIVERSITY OF OKLAHOMA PRESS